PUBLISHED BY

Pedigree®
BOOKS LTD

PEDIGREE BOOKS LTD
BEECH HILL HOUSE
WALNUT GARDENS
ST. DAVIDS HILL
EXETER, DEVON EX4 4DH
shoot@pedigreegroup.co.uk

EDITOR
COLIN MITCHELL

DESIGN
RICHARD GRACE

Living the dream

With the exception of Sir Alex Ferguson at Manchester United, it's not unusual for football managers to be replaced quite often.

It can be pretty similar in the world of magazine editors with the person in the hot seat being changed quite a lot.

When I took over the role of Editor back in summer of 2000 my friends and colleagues were both stunned and envious. The words "a dream job" were often uttered along with a few expletives suggesting how I was a lucky person!

Little did I know at the time what I had let myself in for. I soon discovered that the magazine I occasionally bought as a teenager (many years ago!) was a brand that was bigger than the publication itself.

Shoot holds legendary status and respect among generations of not only its readers but also with thousands of past and present professional footballers who have graced its pages.

In the olden days, when footballers weren't paid a fortune in wages and when they often drank in the pubs with fans, many thought it was the pinnacle of their career to appear on the pages of Shoot.

Our "In Focus" feature is fondly remembered by readers. But for players it took on cult status. In those days many clubs were sent forms for players to fill in about their favourite drink, meal, music, car...even most lusted after woman!

One player told me that he and his fellow pros religiously filled out the forms, sent them back and then every week checked to see if they were the lucky victim of our feature. One even got a right rollicking off his manager for checking Shoot before they went to training.

My journalistic career has involved football for many years but over the past decade the days at Shoot have yielded some

Four decades of fantastic football

MAN HAD JUST LANDED on the moon. England were still World Cup holders. And Shoot was launched onto newsagents' shops.

It was August 1969 when the A4-sized publication kick-started a whole new ball game for football magazines.

The weekly news-magazine with a mixture of colour and black white pictures captured the attention of fans everywhere and became a firm favourite for generations of Dads and Lads

The magazine that swung into action in the Sixties soared into the Seventies; had an exceptional Eighties; did quite nicely in the Nineties and had a new look for the Millennium when it became a monthly.

Now The Voice of Football is leading the field once again by becoming the first football magazine to be only available all around the planet live on the web!

This is not just another football website but a proper magazine where you can actually turn the pages.

Times change. Football has changed. But Shoot is still committed to the best football information around.

Colin Mitchell,
Editor

fantastic, unforgettable and sometimes totally amazing memories.

How many journalists get the chance to exclusively interview **ALAN SHEARER** – a personal hero – sitting on chairs in the middle of a field? How many interview **ROBBIE SAVAGE** and survive?

Then there was the time **STEVEN GERRARD** crashed onto a concrete floor during a photo-shoot (it wasn't our fault, but Gerard Houllier would not have been amused). I'm still not sure if Stevie G convinced me that **DANNY MURPHY** was joking when he asked for his Boyzone CD to be returned.

Arriving in Shoot's former offices with players often turned a few heads too. One girl nearly fainted when she saw **LES FERDINAND** and another just couldn't believe she was in the same lift as **BARRY VENISON**.

ROBBIE KEANE asked for a print from our photo-shoot to send to his Mam back in Dublin – whilst **DAVID JAMES** kidnapped a tray of tea from a hotel waiter so we could have a cuppa as we spoke.

But I will never, ever forget chatting to **BOBBY ROBSON** (just call me Bobby, forget the Sir), one of the nicest and most knowledgeable guys in football. He even remembered my name: "Hello again son, nice to see you."

I'm often asked who is the best, worst or most enjoyable person to interview. I won't tell you the worst, he's still playing! The best is just so difficult to answer but for sheer professionalism, for dedicating a lot of time to me over the years and for being honest and knowing more than you might expect about football in all divisions... it just has to be **MICHAEL OWEN.** Thank you!

The pages of this unique book follow Shoot from the first year to the current day. There have been many changes. No doubt there will be many more to come. But I am certain of one thing – you will be totally entertained and be left wanting more. That's the next goal...

PUTTING SOCCER ON THE MAP

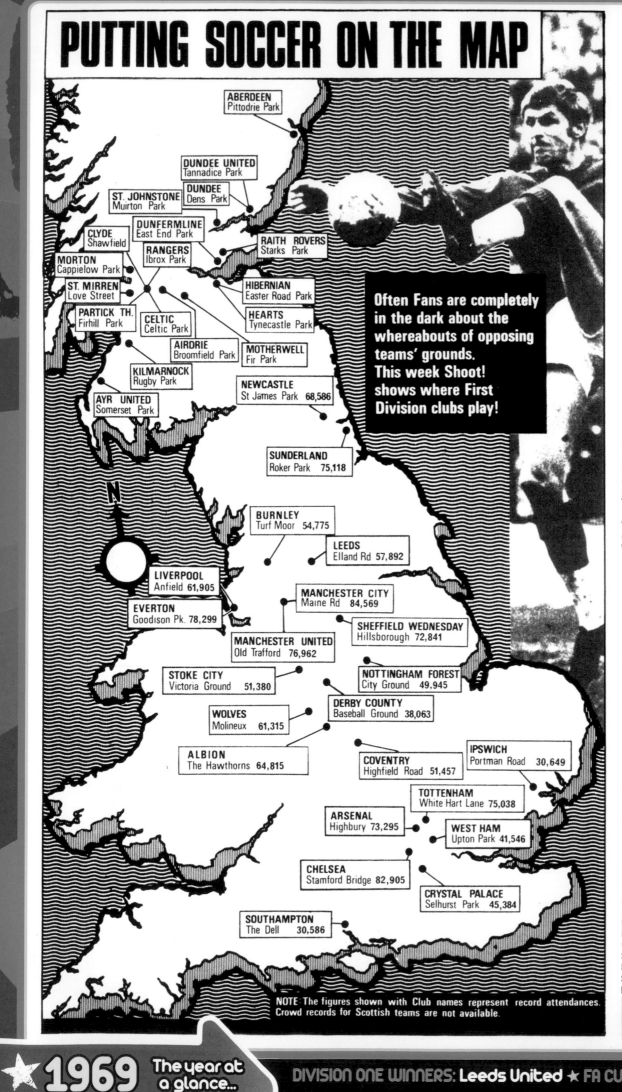

ABERDEEN Pittodrie Park

DUNDEE UNITED Tannadice Park

DUNDEE Dens Park

ST. JOHNSTONE Muirton Park

DUNFERMLINE East End Park

CLYDE Shawfield

RAITH ROVERS Starks Park

RANGERS Ibrox Park

MORTON Cappielow Park

ST. MIRREN Love Street

HIBERNIAN Easter Road Park

PARTICK TH. Firhill Park

CELTIC Celtic Park

HEARTS Tynecastle Park

AIRDRIE Broomfield Park

MOTHERWELL Fir Park

KILMARNOCK Rugby Park

NEWCASTLE St James Park 68,586

AYR UNITED Somerset Park

SUNDERLAND Roker Park 75,118

BURNLEY Turf Moor 54,775

LEEDS Elland Rd 57,892

LIVERPOOL Anfield 61,905

MANCHESTER CITY Maine Rd 84,569

EVERTON Goodison Pk. 78,299

SHEFFIELD WEDNESDAY Hillsborough 72,841

MANCHESTER UNITED Old Trafford 76,962

STOKE CITY Victoria Ground 51,380

NOTTINGHAM FOREST City Ground 49,945

WOLVES Molineux 61,315

DERBY COUNTY Baseball Ground 38,063

ALBION The Hawthorns 64,815

COVENTRY Highfield Road 51,457

IPSWICH Portman Road 30,649

TOTTENHAM White Hart Lane 75,038

ARSENAL Highbury 73,295

WEST HAM Upton Park 41,546

CHELSEA Stamford Bridge 82,905

CRYSTAL PALACE Selhurst Park 45,384

SOUTHAMPTON The Dell 30,586

Often Fans are completely in the dark about the whereabouts of opposing teams' grounds. This week Shoot! shows where First Division clubs play!

NOTE: The figures shown with Club names represent record attendances. Crowd records for Scottish teams are not available.

GUIDE TO THE CLUBS

ALBION (W.B.A.) Formed: 1879. Blue and white stripes; white shorts.
ARSENAL Formed: 1886. Red, white sleeves; white shorts.
BURNLEY Formed: 1881. Claret and sky blue; white shorts.
CHELSEA Formed: 1905. All blue.
COVENTRY Formed: 1883. Sky blue with dark blue and white trims.
CRYSTAL PALACE Formed: 1905. Claret with light blue stripes; white shorts.
DERBY COUNTY Formed: 1884. White; black shorts.
EVERTON Formed: 1878. Royal blue; white shorts.
IPSWICH TOWN Formed: 1880. Royal blue; white shorts.
LEEDS UNITED Formed: 1905. All white.
LIVERPOOL Formed: 1892. Red shirts and shorts.
MANCHESTER CITY Formed: 1880. Sky blue; white shorts.
MANCHESTER UNITED Formed: 1885. Red, white shorts.
NEWCASTLE UNITED Formed: 1882. Black and white stripes; black shorts.
NOTTINGHAM FOREST Formed: 1865. Red, white shorts.
SHEFFIELD WED. Formed: 1866. Royal blue, white sleeves; white shorts.
SOUTHAMPTON Formed: 1885. Red and white stripes; black shorts.
STOKE CITY Formed: 1863. Red and white stripes; white shorts.
SUNDERLAND Formed: 1879. Red and white stripes; white shorts.
TOTTENHAM HOTSPUR Formed: 1882. White; dark blue shorts.
WEST HAM UNITED Formed: 1895. Claret, blue sleeves; white shorts.
WOLVES Formed: 1877. Gold shirts and black shorts.

SCOTTISH LEAGUE

ABERDEEN Formed: 1903. Red shirts and shorts.
AIRDRIEONIANS Formed: 1878. White, red diamond; red shorts.
AYR Formed: 1910. All white.
CELTIC Formed: 1887. Green and white hoops; white shorts.
CLYDE Formed: 1877. Scarlet; black shorts.
DUNDEE Formed: 1893. Dark blue: white shorts.
DUNDEE UNITED Formed: 1910. White and black; white shorts.
DUNFERMLINE Formed: 1907. Black and white stripes; white shorts.
HEARTS Formed: 1873. Maroon; white shorts.
HIBERNIAN Formed: 1875. Green, white sleeves; white shorts.
KILMARNOCK Formed: 1869. Blue and white stripes; white shorts.
MORTON Formed: 1896. Blue and white; white shorts.
MOTHERWELL Formed: 1885. Amber, claret hoop; white shorts.
PARTICK THISTLE Formed: 1876. Red and yellow hoops; white shorts.
RAITH ROVERS Formed: 1883. Navy blue; white shorts.
RANGERS Formed: 1873. Royal blue; white shorts.
ST. JOHNSTONE Formed: 1884. Royal blue; white shorts.
ST. MIRREN Formed: 1876. White, black stripes; white shorts.

NEXT WEEK: GROUNDS OF THE ENGLISH AND SCOTTISH 2ND DIVISION CLUBS.

WANTED

GREAVES J. **HURST G.** **DAVIES R.** **ASTLE J.**

Reward £1,000,000

WATCH out for these four men — they're deadly dangerous! That's the top priority notice every First Division manager is putting out to his defenders!

The reason for concern? The men pictured above are known to shoot on sight — sight of the back of the net, that is, which they are hitting with incredible regularity. And "incredible" is the word — for this is the age of cast-iron defences. Only 1,203 goals were scored in the English First Division last season, **the smallest total for years!**

So that goal-grabbing knack makes sharpshooters the WANTED MEN of soccer . . . wanted by envious managers of rival clubs, of course!

But although the total transfer value of the famous foursome pictured above could soon approach £1,000,000 if the market keeps on spiralling, a fortune isn't likely to tempt their lucky bosses to part with them. After all, money doesn't score goals — our four ace strikers do!

LONE RANGERS

Defenders have the tough assignment of trying to spike these big guns — and others in the high-scoring league. Great goalmen can shoot without warning. They have high-powered ammunition in their feet — and heads that move with the speed of bullets.

The quest for football's wanted men must continue for their greatest "crime" is that they are the lone rangers who can rob rivals of victory.

At the slightest whisper of a sharpshooter ready to give himself up for transfer, a posse of managers will often catch the first train out of town armed with a cheque book and the offer of a long term contract. Before you can say "Goal" a quarry is captured by the man quickest on the draw with his pen.

Jimmy Greaves of the Spurs mob is the defenders' enemy number one. Last season he scored more goals in the Football League than anyone else — 27. He is a crafty, elusive man when he's out goal-poaching and very difficult to shadow.

DRAGNET

Geoff Hurst is known as the "Thunderbolt Hammer" throughout the world by "Intergoal". He is reckoned by many who have dared to face him as the most lethal goalscorer in Britain. Although a closely marked man last season, he still managed to slip the opposition dragnet to fire 25 League goals.

Ron Davies, exiled from Wales, is currently operating at Southampton. Many a crusading back has regretted "going it alone" against him. He spells real trouble for any defender who doesn't take his 20 League goals into account.

Jeff Astle is the "Hawthorn Terror". He's the tearaway leader of the Albion goal-raiders after smash-and-grabbing 21 goals in the League last season. Don't be fooled by that friendly grin — he's another man to be approached with caution at all times.

Big reward money is available in the relentless struggle to hunt down these goal-hungry attackers. Everyone's after them, but they are in short supply. That's why we call them SOCCER'S WANTED MEN!

BOBBY MOORE

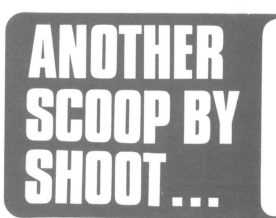

ANOTHER SCOOP BY SHOOT...

SHOOT supporters should be more than satisfied with this week's action-packed issue, because it contains the final set of team-tabs for our superb League Ladders. Through past experience we at SHOOT knew that this gift was sure to be a big hit with fans, although when we decided to offer a second gift as a bonus, we couldn't agree on what form it should take. Then Bobby Moore happened to drop into my office for a conference and one of SHOOT's staffmen suddenly had a brilliant idea — why shouldn't we link the gift with Bobby in some way?

After all, West Ham and England's skipper has won most of the game's great honours — such as Sportsman of the Year, Player of the 1966 World Cup, TV Sports Personality, an O.B.E. — and he's also SHOOT's star writer!

So, to cut a long story short, we're giving away in the next SHOOT a full-colour stand-up model (seven inches high) of Bobby Moore. It's a splendid souvenir of the player who led England to victory in the 1966 World Cup — and who is very likely to repeat the performance in Mexico 1970!

The Editor

writes for you!

❡ The Dressing-Room—WHERE THE GAME IS WON OR LOST! ❡

Manager Frank O'Farrell and his Leicester City lads looking relaxed and happy in the dressing-room. No sign of any nerves here.

THE soccer season is under way and already the players and managers are feeling the strain and tension of this big-time sport as the clubs go into the first bend of the League Championship race.

I'm often told that when I play I appear to be cool, calm and collected — but deep inside, I'm just as keyed-up as the next man.

The time when most players probably feel under the heaviest strain is the hour or so in the dressing-room before a match and sometimes at half-time, too.

What happens then, when the dressing-room is locked to all outsiders? The advice that is given and the exchange of actual ideas during these periods can often win or lose a game.

Immediately before the match, trainers run around making sure their team is happy, managers whisper words of encouragement and run over plans for the last time while players get changed and begin to warm-up.

That's when I begin to feel butterflies in my stomach.

I normally get changed 35 minutes before the kick-off and then have a five or ten minute warm-up session.

Other players get to the ground and strip early. Take Ronnie Boyce, the West Ham midfield player. He likes to be changed at least an hour before the start, and then he potters about in the dressing room doing exercises.

John Charles, the West Ham full-back, always has a massage from the club physiotherapist Rob Jenkins, and Bobby Charlton, when he plays for England, gets a rub down from Harold Shepherdson, the team trainer.

The trainer is the busiest man in the dressing-room before a match. If a key player has only just recovered from an injury, the trainer may still be giving him treatment with only minutes to go.

West Ham take the pre-match hour very seriously. Albert Walker, whose playing career spanned Southport, Bolton Wanderers, Barrow, West Ham, Doncaster and Colchester, is now the Hammers' team attendant.

His match day role is to keep the players at ease. He makes sure everything runs smoothly. For example, when we play an away match he makes arrangements for railway tickets, sees the luggage is on board and tips porters. Albert checks meal times with hotels and, when we are in the dressing-room, he provides the players with bandages, embrocation, chewing gum . . . in fact everything they need. It all helps to make our job easier, leaves us free to concentrate on the game.

When the England team travels abroad — especially to South American and Iron Curtain countries — no detail is too small for attention. We take our own water, boiled sweets and spearmint.

Leeds and England half-back Jackie Charlton is one of the game's many superstitious stars. He likes to be the last player to leave the tunnel. He tells me that's why he refused the Leeds captaincy some time ago when it was a choice between him and Billy Bremner.

Another real England character with a fad about getting ready is Nobby Stiles. Half an hour before kick-off you'll find him jockeying with team-mates, trying to be the last player changed for the match.

England goalkeeper Gordon Banks is a happy-go-lucky type. But he's different before a match. That's when he becomes serious, his mind solely on the job ahead. He has a fairly long warm-up session, doing a lot of bending and stretching exercises and, finally, he goes round the dressing-room shaking hands and wishing everyone good luck.

Players from lower Divisions have nerves, too. Take Watford full-back Duncan Welborne. Some time ago he sent his son to a sweet-shop just round the corner from Watford's ground. Duncan had run out of chewing gum shortly before a home game.

Watford then hit a winning streak. It took them up to Division Two, and Duncan's son still goes to the same sweet-shop for gum just before each home game. But back to the First Division . . .

Alan Mullery, Spurs and England half-back, chats to all his team-mates before a game and tries to make everyone go out feeling like a superman.

Alan likes to talk a lot, though not as much as the greatest

Continued overleaf

'George Best doesn't like to hang about in the dressing-room before the kick-off'

chatter-box of them all — my former West Ham team mate Johnny Byrne, now in South African football. We didn't nickname him "Budgie" without reason!

Jeff Astle did his share, too, in South America on our latest tour. You ask Sir Alf!

I'm told that if George Best arrives in the Old Trafford dressing room at twenty to three he goes out and plays better than if he'd spent an hour preparing for the match. You can have too long to think about the game!

The dressing-room just before a game can be very quiet and very tense. Most of all, I find, players just want to get out on the pitch and kick-off. Half-time is different. If things are going well, everyone is pleased. The winning team try and work out how the losing team will fight back in the second half. The losing side talk about what has gone wrong and how to put it right.

With West Ham and England, both managers — Ron Greenwood and Sir Alf Ramsey — talk a lot during the interval . . . if we are losing.

When it's all over Ron Greenwood keeps his thoughts to himself until the Monday or Tuesday. That's when we next meet for training. He likes to sleep on problems and discuss them later rather than in the heat of the moment directly the game is over.

So there it is — time spent in the dressing-room can often play a big part in the match itself. Some people even say that that is where a game is won or lost!

Until next week then —

The Manchester United and N. Ireland star is shown in his club's second choice strip.

FOCUS

ON
TOM SMITH
LIVERPOOL

IF the name of Tom Smith seems to have been around for some time don't get the impression that Tom is getting old! It's simply that he made his League debut while he was a teenager . . . he's still only 24! The fact that Tom has yet to win a full England cap shows what a wealth of half-back talent manager Sir Alf Ramsey has at his disposal. Tom's forceful play is one of the main reasons for Liverpool's success in recent seasons and he's called the man for whom they invented the term "powerhouse." Certainly those who have seen him play would not argue . . . but the Liverpool fans, in their own sense of Mersey humour, put it like this: "Who needs a defence when you've got Tom in your side?" And there's a rumour around Anfield that Tom practises his slide tackles on a lamp-post! But on the field it's no laughing matter for Tom who regards football as a serious business. He thinks the Liverpool fans are the best in the world and therefore they deserve only the best. And in Tom they have one of the greatest half-backs in Britain . . . the powerhouse of Anfield . . . the pride of the Kop.

FULL NAME: Thomas Smith
BIRTHPLACE: Liverpool
BIRTHDATE: April 5th, 1945
HEIGHT: 5ft 11ins
WEIGHT: 13 st
PREVIOUS CLUBS: None
MARRIED: Yes
CHILDREN: Darren (4 yrs) and Janeatte (18 months)
CAR: Triumph 2000
FAMOUS RELATIONS: None
FAVOURITE PLAYER: Billy Liddell, the former Liverpool and Scotland star.
FAVOURITE OTHER TEAM: Liverpool Reserves
MOST DIFFICULT OPPONENT: Denis Law (Man. Utd.)
MOST MEMORABLE MATCH: 1965 F.A. Cup Final, beating Leeds
BIGGEST THRILL: Scoring against Celtic, Semi-Final 1965-66 European Cup Winners' Cup
BIGGEST DISAPPOINTMENT: Not winning the above competition
BEST COUNTRY VISITED: Switzerland
FAVOURITE FOOD: Steak and scampi
MISCELLANEOUS LIKES: Sitting in the sun with my feet up
MISCELLANEOUS DISLIKES: Snow and ice
FAVOURITE TV SHOW: Rowan & Martin's Laugh-In
FAVOURITE SINGERS: Andy Williams, Dean Martin, Frank Sinatra
FAVOURITE ACTORS/ACTRESSES: Steve McQueen, Sammy Davis Jnr., Shirley Maclaine
BEST FRIENDS: My two children, my wife and my mother
BIGGEST INFLUENCE ON CAREER: Manager Bill Shankly and the Liverpool training staff
BIGGEST DRAG IN SOCCER: The tossing of a coin to decide a European cup tie when the aggregate score is level.
INTERNATIONAL HONOURS: England Youth and Under-23
PERSONAL AMBITION: To be happy and contented
PROFESSIONAL AMBITION: To play for England
IF YOU WEREN'T A FOOTBALLER WHAT DO YOU THINK YOU'D BE?: Probably working in some gloomy office

THE ENGLAND

STEVE PERRYMAN

(Tottenham Hotspur)

❝Banks (Stoke), Wright (Everton), McFarland (Derby), Moore (West Ham), Cooper (Leeds), Mullery (Tottenham), Ball (Everton), Peters (Tottenham), Lee (Manchester City), Hurst (West Ham) and Royle (Everton).

I think Sir Alf Ramsey must start introducing some of the younger talent at his disposal into the England side. And as a build-up for the Munich World Cup I'd like to see Roy McFarland in at centre-half, and Joe Royle at centre-forward. Both players are brilliant . . . and the way Joe Royle played for the Under-23 side the other week, he looks certain for an international place.❞

TO
BY FIVE

On November 25th England start their preparation for the 1974 World Cup Finals with a friendly game against East Germany. This is the first game since the disappointments of Mexico, when Brazil succeeded England as World Champions.

Will Sir Alf Ramsey stick by his estab

BRIAN O'NEIL

(Southampton)

❝Clemence (Liverpool), Madeley (Leeds), Cooper (Leeds), Mullery (Spurs), Lloyd (Liverpool), Hunter (Leeds), Ball (Everton), Channon (S'ton), Royle (Everton), Coates (Burnley), Thompson (Liverpool).

Although we beat Liverpool at The Dell recently, I was most impressed by them. Ray Clemence looked a great prospect and deserves a chance. Larry Lloyd gave Ron (Davies) a hard game — Ron was raving about him after the match. Our Mike Channon is playing well enough to warrant a place — and so is Everton's Joe Royle.❞

★ **1970** The year at a glance...

DIVISION ONE WINNERS: **Everton** ★ FA CUP WINNERS: **Chelsea**

TEAM I'D LIKE SEE PLAYERS

lished stars . . . or will he give youngsters the opportunity to prove themselves?

SHOOT interviewed five top First Division stars and asked what England side they would like to see picked against the East Germans — and found some very interesting formations.

ALAN BIRCHENALL
(Crystal Palace)

❝Banks (Stoke), Wright (Everton), Lloyd (Liverpool), Moore (West Ham), Cooper (Leeds), Ball (Everton), Kember (Crystal Palace), Bell (Manchester City), Jones (Leeds), Royle (Everton), Ian Moore (Nottingham Forest).

That's the side I'd choose . . . very tight at the back, with three non-stop workers in midfield whose distribution is excellent. Steve Kember is playing brilliantly this season and I think he showed his potential in the recent Under-23 international. Up front I'd like to see Joe Royle in the centre, he's a great player . . . so strong and powerful in the air . . . with Mick Jones and Ian Moore as his partners. These three can really score goals. What a side!

Young Larry Lloyd is playing well this season, too, so I think he merits his place in the team, but he'll have to watch out. For my money the best stopper I've seen this year is my team-mate Mel Blyth. He's in superb form. If he keeps it up, then he'll be an international before the end of the season.

I'd be happy with that team — I think Sir Alf Ramsey's got to experiment with youngsters in order to build up a strong squad for the Munich World Cup.❞

BOBBY MONCUR
(Newcastle United)

❝Banks (Stoke), Reaney (Leeds), Cooper (Leeds), Mullery (Spurs), McFarland (Derby), Moore (West Ham), Lee (Manchester City), Ball (Everton), Jones (Leeds), Hughes (Liverpool), Thompson (Liverpool).

You've got to have Banks in goal, no argument there. In the back four, I'd like to see one of the younger centre-halves given a chance —- Roy McFarland, perhaps. Peter Thompson is so good he must be in. He can destroy a team alone. His team-mate Emlyn Hughes is a tremendous worker and would fit in this team. I don't hold much hope for it being picked, though!❞

JIMMY ARMFIELD
(Blackpool)

❝I think Sir Alf Ramsey will treat the international match against East Germany as a prestige game and for that reason I can't see too many changes being made in the England team. Sir Alf believes in settling a side together, and he realises that a lot of changes will disrupt the team. England have an awful lot to play for, they always do . . . and you'll always get people trying to tell Sir Alf who he should pick and why. I'm sure he won't be thinking too much of the future, and he'll want to win this game, so I think you can be sure he'll choose the best side he can to do just that, win the game.

It's not going to be easy — East Germany are a strong side, they are probably the most sports-minded nation in the whole of Europe. One thing's for sure, they'll be supremely fit.

I wouldn't be tied down to selecting an England side, but I'll name some of the players who I see are in with a good chance of playing: **Gordon Banks, Tommy Wright, Terry Cooper, Bobby Moore, Alan Mullery, Martin Peters, Geoff Hurst, Alan Ball, Francis Lee, Colin Bell, Emlyn Hughes, Mick Jones, Allan Clarke, Peter Thompson, Colin Harvey.**

Selecting a centre-half isn't going to be easy. Of course, Bobby Moore has played at number five. But Alf could bring in Manchester United's David Sadler. One thing is certain, though, Derby's Roy McFarland and Liverpool's Larry Lloyd are destined to become internationals in the near future.

England's recent Under-23 game against

West Germany showed us just how good our younger players are . . . and I'm sure players like Joe Royle, Brian Kidd, John Robson, Steve Kember and Peter Shilton must all be in with a chance of selection.

It really all depends on Alf's immediate problems. I can't see him preparing for the 1974 World Cup at this early stage, he'll more likely settle his side for next year's Nations' Cup competition. If his plans are immediate, as I think they will be, then he could be tempted to play Bobby Charlton — he's still a great player with a lot to offer. If not, and he does experiment, then one man I would like to see given a chance is Chelsea's Keith Weller — he's improved in leaps and bounds, and his potential is unlimited. He's Alf's type of player . . . a lot of skill and very hard working.❞

A NINE GOAL THRILLER !!!

JIMMY ARMFIELD, Blackpool skipper and former England international, talks about the greatest match he's ever seen.

"**J**IMMY, what was the greatest match you've seen?" That was the question SHOOT fired at Jimmy Armfield, the former England captain and full-back, and present skipper of Blackpool, now back in the First Division.

Within seconds we had the answer. "An F.A. Cup tie replay between Manchester City and Newcastle at Maine Road way back in 1957 . . . some time in January I think."

Armfield himself has played in more than 600 matches at international, League and Cup level. He has watched countless others, but so deep was the impression left by this game he had no need to search through his memory for the best.

A match which is etched so firmly in the mind must have been a cracker. It was — with nine goals in a see-saw struggle — played in midweek before an audience of 46,990, and few if any of that large number had left the ground before the final whistle shrilled.

WING-WIZARD

"For sheer excitement and enjoyment this was the best," Jimmy enthused. "Yet 48 hours before the kick-off I was not even sure of going. But Bobby Mitchell — what a wing-wizard he was — was in Blackpool with his team-mates and he offered me two tickets. I snapped them up. In fact I took my girl friend Anne (now my wife) along. It was the first match she had seen, and it was so good that it converted her."

The teams had drawn one-all the previous Saturday at St. James's Park, Newcastle, before a gate of 57,980, but there was nothing to suggest, good game though it was, what a thriller the replay would be.

"It was fantastic," says Jimmy. "With ground advantage the City were favourites to win, but they did not expect to bolt into a three-nil interval lead. It looked all over, and although Newcastle had brought hundreds of fans with them, they were subdued. Never before, or since, have I known them so quiet.

"I suppose they were getting ready to drown their sorrows. Then it happened. The transformation was out of this world. Far from giving in The Magpies came out fighting, soon pulled a goal back, then another, and the atmosphere was electric.

"The Geordies were now in full song, willing on their favourites to victory. Another goal, scored I think by winger White, but I am not certain, sent the game into extra-time.

"The rival fans — and the supporters of both clubs are among the most knowledgable in the game — were at fever pitch. After what had gone before I thought that the next goal would prove decisive. How wrong can one be?

"City regained the lead in the first-half of extra-time through Bobby Johnstone to make it 4-3, and quite frankly I thought that was it. I thought that goal had booked their passage into the Fourth Round.

"But thrills and excitement were not yet over. Newcastle fought back brilliantly spurred on by the cheering of their fans and after White had put the teams level, a ginger-haired reserve named Tait slotted in the winner with virtually the last kick.

"It was the first time The Magpies had gone in front, and there was no time for City to hit back . . I suppose a draw would have been a fairer result, but it was a most enjoyable game. One I'll never forget."

But the Cup road ended for Newcastle in the next round, the Fourth, beaten by the odd goal in three by Millwall at The Den.

Bobby Johnstone scored for Manchester City in that thrilling F.A. Cup-tie replay against Newcastle United in 1957.

TONY BROWN
West Bromwich Albion

EVEN though West Brom were knocked out of the F.A. Cup by Sheffield Wednesday last term, their midfield schemer Tony Brown still managed to score what many believe was the goal of the season in that game . . . a volley from 35 yards. But Tony has a habit of scoring goals which, for a midfield man, is a good habit! Signed straight from school, he made his debut for West Brom in 1963 — three days before he signed full professional forms with the club. Originally an inside-forward, Tony made the switch back to wing-half early on in his career and you could say that from then on he's never looked back!

FULL NAME: Anthony Brown
BIRTHPLACE: Oldham
BIRTHDATE: October 3rd, 1945
HEIGHT: 5ft 7½in
WEIGHT: 11st 5lbs
PREVIOUS CLUBS: None
MARRIED: Yes
CHILDREN: None
CAR: Corsair 2000E
FAMOUS RELATIONS: None
FAVOURITE PLAYER: Denis Law
FAVOURITE OTHER TEAM: Manchester United

MOST DIFFICULT OPPONENT: Ray Wilson, ex-Everton
MOST MEMORABLE MATCH: 1967-68 F.A. Cup Final
BIGGEST THRILL: Beating Everton in the above game
BIGGEST DISAPPOINTMENT: Losing to Q.P.R. in the 1966-67 League Cup Final
BEST COUNTRY VISITED: Brazil
FAVOURITE FOOD: Steak and chips; prawn cocktail
MISCELLANEOUS LIKES: Going on holiday with my wife
MISCELLANEOUS DISLIKES: Gardening; traffic jams
FAVOURITE T.V. SHOW: Till Death Us Do Part
FAVOURITE SINGERS: Frank Sinatra, Jose Feliciano
FAVOURITE ACTORS: Steve McQueen, Lee Marvin
BEST FRIEND: My wife
BIGGEST INFLUENCE ON CAREER: Coaching staff at West Brom
BIGGEST DRAG IN SOCCER: Being injured
INTERNATIONAL HONOURS: None
PERSONAL AMBITION: To stay in football for as long as possible.
PROFESSIONAL AMBITION: To play for my country
IF YOU WEREN'T A FOOTBALLER WHAT DO YOU THINK YOU'D BE? Don't know
WHAT PERSON IN THE WORLD WOULD YOU MOST LIKE TO MEET? Frank Sinatra

NORMAN HUNTER (Leeds)

Forwards don't have an easy time these days . . . and here are five good reasons why! We have selected a few of the indestructible players who never let their defences down . . .

SOCCER'S IRON MEN!

If you're a regular reader of our Focus On feature, you will have noticed that when asked their most difficult opponent, many players choose Norman Hunter. Which, of course, is as surprising as rainfall during the English summer! Norman was possibly Leeds' most consistent player last season (Billy Bremner says so) and his crunching tackles constantly ended the dreams of opposing forwards. Blame Bobby Moore if you think that Norman should have won more England caps, but there's one thing that nobody can doubt: he's really a tremendous player!

PETER STOREY (Arsenal)

Charlie George reckons that his toughest opponent is team-mate Peter Storey during five-a-side training sessions! So you can imagine how opposing forwards must find him out on the field. Last season Peter made the transfer from full-back to a defensive midfield man . . . with devastating effect. He won full England international honours last term and is being tipped as a regular in seasons to come.

RON HARRIS (Chelsea)

It wasn't easy to score against The Saints last season, mainly because of the superb form of centre-half John McGrath. Although nearing the end of his career, he is still more than a match for forwards — as they found out last term. With Southampton in Europe next season, fans at The Dell are hoping John can re-produce last season's form against some of the Continent's top sides. John told us that he's keeping his fingers crossed . . . to keep forwards out!

JOHN McGRATH (Southampton)

"How Ron has never played for England I'll never know. He's been one of the most consistent defenders in the country over the past five years." The words of Chelsea boss Dave Sexton . . . sentiments that are echoed by thousands of Chelsea fans. They reckon their iron man ought to wear the white of England as well as the blue of Chelsea. But as long as "Buller" does his stuff for The Blues, Chelsea supporters won't mind too much.

TOM SMITH (Liverpool)

His Manager Bill Shankly is happy now. Tom won his so-deserved England cap last season. "Not the last, I hope," growls "Shanks" with a grin! Tom is probably the player for whom the nickname "power-house" was created. To say he makes his tackles felt is an understatement . . . but he is fair. He knows only one way to play: hard. Every team needs a Tom Smith in their side. But there's only one original model. Lucky, lucky Liverpool!

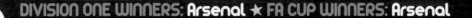

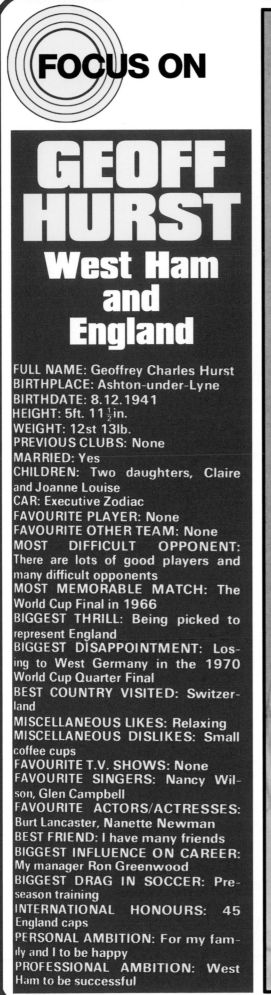

FOCUS ON

GEOFF HURST
West Ham and England

FULL NAME: Geoffrey Charles Hurst
BIRTHPLACE: Ashton-under-Lyne
BIRTHDATE: 8.12.1941
HEIGHT: 5ft. 11½in.
WEIGHT: 12st 13lb.
PREVIOUS CLUBS: None
MARRIED: Yes
CHILDREN: Two daughters, Claire and Joanne Louise
CAR: Executive Zodiac
FAVOURITE PLAYER: None
FAVOURITE OTHER TEAM: None
MOST DIFFICULT OPPONENT: There are lots of good players and many difficult opponents
MOST MEMORABLE MATCH: The World Cup Final in 1966
BIGGEST THRILL: Being picked to represent England
BIGGEST DISAPPOINTMENT: Losing to West Germany in the 1970 World Cup Quarter Final
BEST COUNTRY VISITED: Switzerland
MISCELLANEOUS LIKES: Relaxing
MISCELLANEOUS DISLIKES: Small coffee cups
FAVOURITE T.V. SHOWS: None
FAVOURITE SINGERS: Nancy Wilson, Glen Campbell
FAVOURITE ACTORS/ACTRESSES: Burt Lancaster, Nanette Newman
BEST FRIEND: I have many friends
BIGGEST INFLUENCE ON CAREER: My manager Ron Greenwood
BIGGEST DRAG IN SOCCER: Pre-season training
INTERNATIONAL HONOURS: 45 England caps
PERSONAL AMBITION: For my family and I to be happy
PROFESSIONAL AMBITION: West Ham to be successful

★ LEAGUE CUP WINNERS: Tottenham ★ HIT RECORD: T Rex - Hot Love

GEORGE BEST continues to recall the times when he hit the headlines in his colourful career . . .

'MY FIRST-TEAM DEBUT WAS A SECRET'

YOU LEFT me last week, I hope you'll remember, gazing at the team noticeboard at Old Trafford and finding that I'd been picked in the first-team party for the first time, but only as a reserve.

Well, I figured, that's better than nothing. I'd been a full-time professional for the best part of four months, spending most of it on holiday and the rest of it trying to turn on the odd bit of magic in front of small crowds for the Central League side or junior teams.

However, it was Friday, September the 13th — and the game the following day was against West Bromwich Albion. Just seeing my name up there on the team-list, reserve or not (and don't forget we didn't have substitutes in those days) was a thrill. Then I managed to behave in the way that makes so many people despair of me having any sense at all.

What had at first been a real HIGHLIGHT of my young life, suddenly changed. I had this idea that I was going to be left without a game on that Saturday. And rather than just idle around while the first-team played the Midlanders, I'd rather have been on active service with one of the junior sides.

But I reckoned without the can-niness of Matt Busby. Now I've said many times how he's helped me at different stages of my career, but this was one occasion when he really showed why he was a master handler of men, a super-manager — and that's not taking into account that he was also a brilliant club and Scottish footballer!

Matt knew darned well that I'd be playing in the first-team. He had Ian Moir named as outside-right, but he was injured — nothing much but enough to keep him out. But instead of naming me outright as the replacement, Matt helped me get a full night's sleep by hinting that my services probably wouldn't be required.

Of course, any player remembers his first full-professional game. I was shoved in against Graham Williams, a Welsh international who was reckoned to have one of the hardest tackles in the game. When I was reminded of this by some of my team-mates, notably Nobby Stiles who wore the number eight shirt that day and Paddy Crerand . . . well, I suppose I was a bit cocky and I said: "Ah, but he's got to catch up with me first."

The game was okay. We won 1-0. Dave Sadler, who was in digs with me at Mrs. Mary Fullaway's house, scored our goal. I got a knock on the ankle and Matt moved me over to the left-wing. Things fell into place and my only regret was people might have thought I was switched to the other wing to keep me out of harm's way . . . or at least Graham Williams' way!

That evening I got the local evening paper and was knocked out to read that I was "an exciting prospect to brighten up even the dullest of games."

Denis Law wasn't in the side that day, but I'd had my first taste of soccer in the big-time, and I looked forward to one day linking up with the famous Scotsman who had long been another hero figure to me.

Now some players can look back on a game and virtually tell you kick by kick what happened. I'm not like that. I remember the occasion, obviously . . .

"I didn't fancy playing against Graham Williams (left). He had a reputation for being a hard tackler."

What I remember more was the business of actually getting to Old Trafford to even start the game. It was one of those days when people would be better off on the beach, or playing cricket — if people are still interested in playing that amazingly boring game! Oh, I suppose playing cricket ON the beach would be an ideal way of spending the afternoon.

But I was up bright and early, which was mainly due to people wanting space in the bathroom! I got to the ground about 11.30 a.m. and was caught up in what then was the United match-day ritual . . . on to Davyhulme Golf Club for lunch.

But bear in mind I thought I was merely reserve. Paddy Crerand actually told me that I was in and Ian Moir was out. So that was why a lot of people around the club, blokes on the staff, were wishing me the very BEST of luck! I thought they were kicking up a bit too much fuss about simply being twelfth man!

And I guarantee I was the most frightened lad in Manchester when first I heard about Graham Williams' fearsome reputation. Later, as I said earlier, I found some cockiness from somewhere deep inside me!

We had our steaks and toast and the last game of snooker or cards or what-have-you. What I had was an hour or two of staring into space and wondering if all was going to go well.

Most of all, though, I can remember arriving at the ground in the United team coach, and seeing all those fans just looking, or staring, or waving good luck wishes. And it was obvious to me that most of them were eyeing me and wondering just who on earth I was. Don't forget they also didn't know that I was to replace Ian Moir.

What was actually happening at Old Trafford that season was that some of the "older" players were being left out to make way for the younger men. The club lost out to Everton in the Charity Shield game, I remember. Chaps like Albert Quixall, David Herd, and Johnny Giles were being omitted.

LEEDS STAR

Giles? Yes, Johnny Giles, who is now with Leeds United and one of the best midfield generals in the business. He's been around quite a while, has Johnny.

Among the players who'd been drafted in were Sammy McMillan, another Irish kid, and Phil Chisnall and Ian Moir whom I'd now replaced. It was a sort of rebuilding scene, and I felt very good indeed to be part of it, even if I wasn't much more than one brick in the plan of things.

It'd be marvellous to report that I played so well against West Brom that I stayed in the team and was happy ever after. But things certainly rarely work out like that in professional soccer. In fact, I was dropped for the very next game!

No, it was nothing to do with the way I'd played. Just that Ian Moir was fit again and deserved to get his place back. As a matter of fact, my career did get turned upside down a bit, because I somehow slid back to the fourth team for a while.

Not only because of this phase of my life, but for things that have happened since, you learn fast that you can be leaping for joy one moment and then weeping with sorrow the next. I felt bad about being relegated to the lower sides simply because I knew that my mates back home in Belfast would be taking the mickey. They'd barely got over their astonishment when I actually ran away from Old Trafford because apparently I preferred to be with my mum!

But that Christmas I was recalled from Belfast, where I'd been celebrating very quietly indeed — I felt like a fallen idol — and played against Burnley. And we won 5-1 and I got my first goal. Willie Anderson — now with Aston Villa — played in that one, too, and both of us held our places for a while.

The young lads were coming through, thick and fast. And here I'd like to just spare a thought for Bobby Noble, a fine full-back who had been with most of us lads in the United side which won the F.A. Youth Cup. A dreadful car accident put him out, once and for all, from the big-time.

SCRAPBOOK

My scrapbook back home in Belfast has a few pictures of that victorious young side. Jimmy Rimmer; Duff and Noble at fullback; then John Fitzpatrick along with Farrar and McBride; and a forward-line of Willie Anderson, myself, Dave Sadler, Albert Kinsey and Johnny Aston. Dave Sadler was a goal-getter in those days, you see.

That was a highlight in my life,

"It was Paddy Crerand (above) who first told me I was in against West Brom. I took the place of the injured Ian Moir."

George Best

"Matt Busby was cunning about me making my debut. He actually hinted that I wouldn't be in the first-team."

THREEPWOOD

27

TOP OF PAGE . . . The Wilsons recently moved to a beautiful house in Herts. They were waiting to greet our photographer.

INSET . . . . Bob hard at work answering his fan mail — with a copy of SHOOT by his side, of course!

LEFT . . . Four of Bob's honours — (from left) League Champions' Plaque, Fairs Cup Trophy, a special tankard for winning The Double in 1971, and his F.A. Cup winners' medal.

RIGHT . . . Arsenal reported back for pre-season training on Tuesday (July 25th), but Bob's children obviously think he needs extra practice as well!

LEFT . . . Bob is a regular contributor to B.B.C. Television's football coverage and has special equipment at home to enable him to prepare his soccer spots. We see Bob with some recordings of "Match of the Day", which he was about to analyse for points which may have gone unnoticed during the game. Bob's strength is to tell viewers about the finer arts of football, and it is something he does extremely well.

BELOW . . . Two of Bob's most treasured shirts — the Scottish jersey he wore on his international debut, and the one he used during the triumphant F.A. Cup Final against Liverpool (right).

at home with the stars

THIS WEEK: BOB WILSON ARSENAL

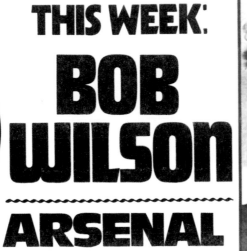

RIGHT . . . Bob's house has a huge garden, which proves very popular with his children John, Robert and Anna . . . not to mention their Golden Labrador, Misty. Here, Bob and his attractive wife, Megs, relax with their family and enjoy the summer sunshine.

FIRST DIVISION

Leeds United

I'VE waited five years to get my hands on a League Championship medal. Now, at last, I can proudly add one to my collection.

With a spot of luck, I wouldn't have had to wait that long. Leeds have been so near to winning the title since I joined the club in the summer of 1969. Before the season just ended, they'd been runners-up three out of the previous four campaigns.

Yet, becoming this season's Champions was in some ways an anti-climax. I didn't expect Liverpool to be beaten at home by Arsenal three days before our final League game at Q.P.R.

'Pool losing meant we became Champs without everything hinging on our last match.

'We've also won friends'

by striker Allan Clarke

Nevertheless, we didn't relax, beating Rangers 1-0, and I would like to think that everyone present felt that we played like worthy Champions.

Leeds won the title because they are the finest outfit in the League. And, for a change, the team got the right publicity. It was thoroughly deserved.

We've always tried to play attacking football and I reckon I can safely say that during 1973-74 the club won the nation over with its particular brand of soccer.

We also got some good breaks, and the general feeling was that it would have been a shame had we not clinched the title.

Even a former neighbour of mine, and a fanatical Liverpool supporter, said he was pleased for us!

On reflection, the amount of injuries we had during the season could have ruined all our hopes and plans. The team was unchanged for about the first seven matches. From then on at least one key player was missing each week.

It says a great deal for the character of our established players, and the men who stood in for them. They did a first-class job.

My own form? I was dogged for about two months by ligament trouble in my right knee and ankle. I played when I shouldn't have done. But I still managed 16 goals, although any striker will admit that he's never satisfied with his own personal tally, whatever the reason.

Adapting

No special tactics were employed to enable Leeds to avoid defeat until their 30th match. We always play it simple, sizing up the opposition during the first five to ten minutes of each match, then adapting ourselves accordingly. Besides, no one at Leeds knows what the meaning of defeat is.

There was a period during March when I thought we'd be caught. In two successive matches we lost 1-0 at Liverpool and 4-1 at home to Burnley.

The latter was a terrible defeat. We had 80 per cent of the play, but didn't get the breaks.

I've never been in a Leeds side beaten so heavily at home. In fact, according to the record books, their last similar defeat was around 12 years ago when the club was still in the Second Division.

After that Burnley match we were written off. I wish some people would take into account that players don't lose their skills, only matches . . . and we don't lose many of them.

Last Chance

Next season, of course, Leeds carry England's banner in the European Cup. We've only qualified for this competition once before. That was in 1969-70 when Celtic knocked us out in the Semi-Finals.

I feel this is the last chance for the present squad to win Europe's premier trophy. We're now at our peak, but aren't getting any younger.

We can all remember our previous failure and are determined that 1974-75 will see us succeed to become only the second English club to win the European Cup.

It's always been an ambition of mine to gain a winners' medal in this tournament. I'm confident this time next year I'll be the delighted owner of one.

MODESTY they say is a hallmark of greatness. If that's so then Southampton and England superstar Mike Channon is simply great.

But you don't have to be a budding Sherlock Holmes to arrive at that conclusion. For there can be few arguments that modest Mike is in the highest class when it comes to goalscoring.

His record speaks for itself and his 11 appearances in the white shirt of England have boosted 24-year-old Channon into the world-class ratings. Channon, though, has remained quiet and unassuming despite his meteoric climb to stardom and is philosophical about his success.

He tells SHOOT about the breaks that helped him into the big-time.

'THE MOST EXCITING FORWARD IN EUROPE'

That's how highly Southampton General-Manager Ted Bates regards his young striker

MIKE CHANNON

"My first and most important chance came when I was just 15. For it was then that I signed for The Saints and believe me that was the real break that helped make Mike Channon.

"I signed along with seven other young hopefuls and you can see the luck I've had in making the grade, when you realise that of the eight only myself and full-back Bob McCarthy still remain at The Dell.

"I even scored on my first-team debut, which when you're a striker like me, is as good a break as you can have. That goal came in a 2-2 draw against Bristol City over the vital Easter period leading up to when Southampton were promoted to the First Division in 1966.

"Moving on a few years, another break came my way while I was playing for England.

"That was in February last year when we 'sassenachs' took the Scotland side to the cleaners to the tune of 5-0 at Hampden. I scored one of our goals and since then I've not looked back.

"In fact, I have missed only one international since then and that was when we went down 2-0 in a World Cup game against Poland at Katowice last June.

"As a chap with a burning ambition to appear in the world's major soccer tournament, I was deeply disappointed we didn't qualify for this year's World Cup Finals.

"But there is always Argentina in 1978 and I hope to be in the England side that goes some way to making up for this year's failure.

"Before then there is the European Championship (Nations Cup) in 1976 and that will give us something to play for.

"If I can help England set up a faith-restoring victory, that will be fine. A win would give us all — players and fans — some compensation for our World Cup exit."

But modesty or not, with Mike still in his early 20's, and with Peter Osgood now to help him, have we yet seen the best of Channon?

Southampton's General-Manager Ted Bates, the man who groomed Channon to greatness, thinks not.

"We will see Mike improve over the next few years," he says. "By the time the next World Cup comes along in 1978, Mike will be at his peak. He is the most exciting forward in Europe.

"But he can still improve. I think he can work on his reactions in the box. If he improves there — and he is working on it — he can score another ten goals a season.

"He is modest all right but on the pitch he's ruthless. He always looks for the ball and not the man. That's why he's priceless."

SUPERMAC'S TARGETS

MACDONALD'S GOALSCORING CAREER

	Appearances	Goals
Fulham	10 (3 sub)	5
Luton	88	49
Newcastle	148	76
(Football League only)		
England	11	6

NEWCASTLE United's Malcolm Macdonald is as fearless in making soccer predictions as he is at running at defences — and pulls no punches in assessing his own and United's chances of success this season.

Malcolm says: "Instead of aiming at a target of 30 goals as I have done for the past two seasons, I'm confidently expecting to hit 35 before next May.

"And I also believe that Newcastle can overcome their biggest bogey, inconsistency, to go on and make a serious bid for the League Championship.

"The incentive to put an end to the in - and - out displays typical of United for so long must come from the boardroom rather than the dressing-room. And our new manager, Gordon Lee, has convinced me he can transmit his own determination to the players."

So immediate has been the impact of Lee that Macdonald, not the easiest of persons to impress, noticed the difference in atmosphere during the first week of training.

"Supercharged"

"The air has been supercharged and there is a completely new enthusiasm among the players since Mr Lee has taken over our coaching sessions," said Macdonald. "I know most clubs are optimistic in July and August, but I feel something much more than just optimism.

"Already, the lads are beginning to believe in themselves, and if they carry this feeling into every game we can win the title. The Championship is not the Everest it used to be. Take Derby County for instance. After they won it, it gave hope to the underdogs and outsiders."

In Macdonald's view, the contenders for the title who will not be outsiders are inevitably Liverpool and Leeds United. He says: "They can never be written off — but along with them and Newcastle, I expect Stoke, Ipswich and Derby to be in with a good chance."

If Malcolm demonstrates team-spirit by having confidence in the ability of his colleagues, he makes no bones about his personal approach to goalscoring. He sums it up: "To get goals, it is necessary to be totally selfish in the opposing penalty-area.

"But if by doing so I can score enough goals to help Newcastle collect honours, then my single-minded approach will have paid off."

Then moving on from club level to international, the Newcastle sharpshooter disclosed his feelings on playing centre-forward for England. He said: "My ambition is to prove to everybody that I am good enough to be rated a regular choice for my country.

"Last season I reckon I broke the ice by getting among the goals. Now it is up to me to go all out this term to make the centre-forward position my own for England."

'UNITED WILL WIN SOMETHING'

THEY were not one of the country's best supported clubs . . . they didn't grab many headlines . . . and not many people tipped them to win honours.

Yet, there is no doubt Sheffield United were the First Division's shock team last season, and are undoubtedly already being taken much more seriously this term.

According to their brilliant England midfield star Tony Currie, the pundits will be well advised to keep United in mind when making predictions.

Currie, of the swerving hips and flowing passes, believes United — for so long totally overshadowed by Yorkshire rivals Leeds — will cause even more of a surprise this season and will be challenging for glory all the way.

But he also thinks they must first conquer the one fault that let them down during the last campaign — inconsistency.

Says Tony, acknowledged as being one of the most elegant players in the game today: "We certainly caused a few raised eyebrows throughout the land by finishing sixth, just four points behind Champions Derby.

"I don't think many people outside the club ever thought we would finish so high in the table.

"After all, we had several clubs with more glamorous names, like Leeds, Manchester City, West Ham, Arsenal and Spurs, finishing below us and the way we were playing it was a shame the season ended when it did.

"We lost only two of our last 15 matches and were going so strongly it would have been interesting to see where we would have finished if the campaign had lasted just another month.

"It was no fluke, either. We really hit top form after the turn of the year and I believe we were one of the most attractive sides in the First Division.

"What let us down in the end was our inconsistent start. And we didn't do too well away from home, either.

"We lost only two games all season at Bramall Lane, but were beaten nine times on our travels, and you don't win titles with form like that.

'Stronger Away'

"Our manager, Ken Furphy, and all the players are aware of the problem and I feel we'll be much stronger away from home this season.

"Our 1-1 draw with Derby at Bramall Lane in the opening match was just the result we needed. In fact the Champions were lucky to escape with a point.

"Unfortunately, we slipped back three days later by losing 3-1 to Arsenal again at home.

"Despite that setback I still think we will give the fans plenty to cheer about. No other team will have an easy time against us — believe me.

"After all, we have some terrific players — like goalkeeper Jim Brown, Tony Field, and the ever-dangerous Alan Woodward — and we really believe in ourselves.

"And we're hoping Chris Guthrie, our close-season signing from Southend, will add bite to our attack because we need to score more goals.

"All things considered, I'm sure we are going to have another great season and perhaps even win something. That is what we really want. United are overdue for a success."

Currie also has a personal ambition to spur him forward this season — to win a regular England place.

TOMMY Docherty's men may have missed out on the F.A. Cup and the Football League Championship last season — but when it came to support, there was no one to match Manchester United.

In a year when gates generally were slumping again, to a post-War low of 24,896,053, a drop of nearly 700,000 for the season, support for the exciting football flowing from the talented young United side, simply soared.

They were not merely the only club in the country to attract more than one million fans to their 21 home matches in the First Division, but they boosted their average to a remarkable 54,750, the highest by any club since United's own figures of 57,759, during 1967-68.

Standing on the terraces, or even sitting in the stand at Old Trafford, is not just watching a football match but a memorable experience and, looked at in more detail, United's crowd figures are quite astonishing.

For instance, if you isolate the second-half of the season, when it became clear Martin Buchan and his brilliant team-mates were chasing a League and Cup double so soon after hauling themselves out of the Second Division, the average rose to an incredible 58,053.

It was the fourth year running and the eighth time in the past ten years United have finished top of the crowd tables.

It is easy to understand why manager Docherty, while critical of the hooligan fringe whose frighten-

Attendances in the FOOTBALL LEAGUE 1975-76

MAN. UNITED — CHAMPION CROWD-PULLERS

Manchester United's Steve Coppell takes on and beats Q.P.R. defenders Ron Abbott (left) and Dave Webb at Old Trafford on January 10th. United won 2-1, roared on by a crowd of 58,312.

ing outbursts cause anguish and damage wherever they seem to go and give the club a bad name, salutes the majority as "the finest supporters in the land".

League Champions, Liverpool, the only club to break United's domination of the gate tables in the past ten years, trailed way behind this time, their average down by more than 4,000 when United's was up by 6,000.

Worked out over the season it meant United's home matches attracted 275,666 more people than the Kop at Anfield.

Despite the Championship near-miss by Queens Park Rangers and the agonising drama of Crystal Palace's failure to achieve what at one time had seemed likely to be certain promotion from the Third Division, London suffered badly in terms of crowds, reflecting an overall loss of 166,505.

Chelsea, down by 177,235, were hardest hit — Rangers up by 72,000 enjoyed the biggest boom.

The biggest increase in the country was at Villa Park, where the return to the First Division meant an extra 235,000 customers for Aston Villa.

The biggest drop was at Everton,

DIVISION ONE

	Total	Average	1974-5 Average	Total Gains or losses
Arsenal	565,851	26,945	28,315	− 28,764
Aston Villa	816,355	38,874	27,654	+ 235,616
Birmingham	588,062	28,002	30,854	− 59,873
Burnley	380,514	18,119	19,641	− 5,960
Coventry	406,779	19,370	19,100	+ 5,675
Derby	595,535	28,358	26,718	+ 34,441
Everton	569,414	27,114	40,020	− 271,026
Ipswich	532,688	25,366	24,924	+ 9,281
Leeds	661,739	31,511	34,821	− 69,518
Leicester	463,033	22,049	23,765	− 36,032
Liverpool	874,085	41,623	45,966	− 91,201
Man. City	719,878	34,279	32,898	+ 20,012
Man. Utd.	1,149,751	54,750	48,388	+ 133,588
Middlesbrough	487,687	23,223	29,970	− 141,701
Newcastle	694,258	33,059	34,613	− 32,634
Norwich	477,952	22,759	22,460	+ 6,287
Q.P.R.	500,849	23,849	20,393	+ 72,582
Sheff. Utd	494,539	23,549	22,555	+ 20,880
Stoke	468,595	22,314	27,011	− 98,645
Tottenham	584,566	27,836	26,457	+ 28,953
West Ham	575,757	27,417	29,872	− 51,960
Wolves	481,974	22,951	23,404	− 9,523

DIVISION TWO

	Total	Average	1974-5 Average	Total Gains or losses
Blackburn	220,271	10,489	12,650	− 70,694
Blackpool	174,451	8,307	10,112	− 37,901
Bolton	407,200	19,390	13,799	+ 111,403
Bristol City	340,281	16,203	14,060	+ 45,006
Bristol Rov.	210,458	10,021	12,222	− 46,208
Carlisle	173,859	8,279	14,529	− 131,265
Charlton	244,217	11,629	10,448	+ 4,006
Chelsea	398,088	18,956	27,396	− 177,235
Fulham	204,556	9,740	10,808	− 22,431
Hull	144,927	6,901	8,572	− 35,098
Luton	222,332	10,587	17,396	− 142,988
Nott'm. For.	268,908	12,805	12,999	− 4,083
Notts County	260,703	12,414	10,927	+ 31,235
Oldham	219,584	10,456	12,492	− 42,750
Orient	134,100	6,385	7,604	− 25,598
Oxford	141,464	6,736	8,260	− 32,009
Plymouth Argyle	310,804	14,800	14,060	− 12,585*
Portsmouth	219,917	10,472	12,474	− 42,043
Southampton	370,603	17,647	15,909	+ 36,498
Sunderland	656,259	31,250	29,931	+ 27,697
West Brom	361,752	17,226	12,424	+ 100,847
York	113,673	5,413	8,954	− 74,371

*Plymouth show overall loss despite increased average because previous season in Third Division they played two extra matches.

down by 271,000, and it was the combined impact of losing both Aston Villa and Manchester United which accounted for a sharp fall in Second Division total attendances. The figure of 5,798,405 was down by more than 1m.

Increased admission prices, at a time of added unemployment, was one obvious factor for the overall slump in soccer attendances last season, coupled with ever-increasing travelling costs to matches.

The saddest aspect of this was that the financial squeeze coincided with a season in which the clubs, in the main, offered customers a much more attractive entertainment package with the number of goals fractionally up.

At least things were a little brighter at the lowest level, with Fourth Division gates up by nearly ten per cent thanks principally to Doncaster Rovers, Lincoln, Northampton and Reading.

Lincoln's gates, in winning the Fourth Division, were higher than Hereford's who won the Third, although Crystal Palace's average of 20,123 in the Third Division not only exceeded everyone bar Sunderland in the Second Division, but illustrated greater support than for Burnley and Coventry in the First Division.

Palace, like Manchester United, however, found these healthy and stimulating statistics little comfort when set against the prizes which slipped from their grasp.

LINCOLN LEAD THE 'FOURTH'

Above: Lincoln skipper Sam Ellis greets his side's second goal against Doncaster at Sincil Bank on Easter Saturday. Lincoln won 5-0 in front of 14,096 fans.

Left: Sunderland's Billy Hughes beats this tackle by a Portsmouth defender at Roker Park in April. Sunderland won 2-0 to clinch the Second Division title . . . 40,515 was the official attendance.

Right: Stewart Jump of Crystal Palace in action during the vital promotion clash v. Millwall at Selhurst Park on March 30th. Over 38,000 fans witnessed an exciting 0-0 draw.

SUNDERLAND TOP THE 'SECOND'

PALACE — KINGS OF THE 'THIRD'

DIVISION THREE

	Total	Average	1974-5 Average	Total gains or losses
Aldershot	105,501	4,587	4,384	+ 4,652
Brighton	352,891	15,343	11,750	+ 82,624
Bury	136,518	5,935	5,527	− 9,396
Cardiff City	269,146	11,702	9,143	+ 77,133
Chester	117,360	5,102	4,744	+ 8,230
Chesterfield	113,129	4,918	4,614	− 6,994
Colchester	77,015	3,348	5,129	− 40,953
Crystal Pal.	462,849	20,123	17,273	+ 65,549
Gillingham	144,922	6,300	7,331	− 23,697
Grimsby	128,344	5,580	5,962	− 8,783
Halifax Town	57,643	2,506	2,681	− 4,028
Hereford	190,280	8,273	7,230	+ 23,983
Mansfield	168,921	7,344	7,203	+ 11,154
Millwall	176,843	7,688	8,582	− 5,283
Peterboro'	174,951	7,606	8,446	− 19,317
Port Vale	95,062	4,133	4,346	− 4,898
Preston	162,596	7,069	9,567	− 57,458
Rotherham	120,034	5,218	5,487	− 6,182
Sheff. Wed.	258,038	11,219	13,453	− 24,478
Shrewsbury	106,989	4,651	4,124	+ 12,116
Southend	115,242	5,010	6,654	− 37,821
Swindon	177,417	7,713	8,280	− 13,032
Walsall	141,110	6,135	6,268	− 3,064
Wrexham	95,648	4,158	4,376	− 5,001

DIVISION FOUR

	Total	Average	1974-5 Average	Total gains or losses
AFC Bournemouth	102,600	4,460	5,987	− 35,118
Barnsley	85,280	3,707	4,645	− 21,571
Bradford City	67,073	2,916	3,190	− 6,309
Brentford	117,218	5,096	5,171	− 1,728
Cambridge	59,018	2,560	3,021	− 10,467
Crewe	54,601	2,373	2,648	− 6,322
Darlington	51,223	2,227	2,233	− 147
Doncaster	139,297	6,056	2,974	+ 70,879
Exeter	75,064	3,263	3,435	− 3,950
Hartlepool	50,194	2,182	2,633	− 10,384
Huddersfield	124,900	5,430	5,427	+ 61
Lincoln City	193,230	8,401	5,794	+ 59,946
Newport Co	47,844	2,080	2,717	− 14,667
Northampton	147,560	6,415	4,178	+ 51,828
Reading	176,936	7,692	5,385	+ 53,067
Rochdale	36,665	1,594	1,506	+ 2,015
Scunthorpe	70,090	3,047	2,239	+ 18,583
Southport	33,323	1,448	1,736	− 6,623
Stockport	74,474	3,238	2,099	+ 26,189
Swansea	67,435	2,931	2,070	+ 19,817
Torquay	60,725	2,640	2,868	− 5,243
Tranmere	89,235	3,879	2,803	+ 24,764
Watford	106,000	4,608	6,460	− 42,583
Workington	29,353	1,276	1,481	− 4,710

'My PRESENT from Rangers'

TARTAN TALK
John Greig

CHRISTMAS came early for yours truly this year when Rangers announced they were going to give me a testimonial game. Okay, I know these sort of matches are almost commonplace these days, but I admit I was overwhelmed by the gesture.

Why? Simply because I am the first-ever player to be granted a testimonial by Rangers, and when you look through our past and see some of the great names that is really astonishing.

I am staggered by this move by Rangers. Honestly, even now I don't think I can fully take it all in. I haven't even thought about the financial side of it yet. A sum of £50,000 has been mentioned. Incredible!

I've always been happy to play

for Rangers and let the cash take care of itself. Obviously, money is extremely important to everyone with a family — or without, for that matter — but I don't think I could ever be accused of being money-mad.

It's been a privilege just pulling on that blue jersey on match day. I'll always get a kick out of that. I've never lost my enthusiasm for the game, and when you are playing for a club like Rangers you realise just how lucky you are.

There have been many loyal servants with other clubs who have never had the rewards they have been due. Things have gone right for me and I realise just how lucky I am.

John Greig believes that if Jim Baxter (right) had stayed with the club he might have had a testimonial.

Let's look at some of the players in the past who might have been given a testimonial. There's Willie Waddell, for a start. He came into the Rangers side as a teenager and I have never heard him being accused of ever giving anything less than 100 per cent effort.

And what about Jim Baxter? If he had stayed with Rangers no one surely could have begrudged him a big financial send-off. Bobby Shearer was the captain of Rangers before I took over and he, too, gave his all for the club.

He was loyal to the side and I've often heard it said that Bobby would

have tackled King Kong in the cause of Rangers. I wouldn't disagree with that. Yes, there are so many players down through the years who could have been honoured, but weren't.

Don't get me wrong, though. Rangers have always looked after their players, but they have never done it in the manner of a testimonial. That is why I am so overwhelmed.

Which team would I like to provide the opposition? Any team! There have been a lot of names flying about, but the main thing is to have a side that plays football and allows us to play our game. Then the fans will see a really entertaining clash.

Queens Park Rangers have been mentioned as possibles and I certainly wouldn't argue with that. It would be good to play against my old Scottish mate Frank McLintock. It's great to see Frank doing so well with the Loftus Road men. Critics thought he was finished when Arsenal allowed him to go, but he has proved them all wrong.

Youngster

In fact, when I come to think of it, I'm just a youngster compared to Frank! Sorry, Frank, you know I'm only joking!

I've seen Q.P.R. on the telly and they have always looked a good, attractive side. Stan Bowles has an amazing assortment of tricks, hasn't he? I wouldn't mind trying to get to grips with him.

And, of course, there's Don Masson in the middle of the park. Don deserves all the praise that comes his way. He is a classy player and he has brought flair to Scotland's midfield.

Anyway, like I said earlier, I wouldn't mind playing against Q.P.R., but the decision is not mine. I'm just happy to be in this position . . . now I really do believe in Santa Claus!

I'll sign off now by wishing everyone a very merry Christmas. I won't be here next week, of course, so I'll take this opportunity of also saying a happy New Year to all SHOOT/GOAL readers. I hope your favourite team does well in 1977 — and if they happen to wear light blue jerseys and play at Ibrox then I'll be doubly pleased!

John Greig

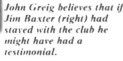

When team-mate Bobby Lennox broke an ankle, one of the first players to him was Roy Aitken (below, number six).

Roddy MacDonald's (above) fine form this term has allowed Aitken more freedom in midfield.

son. Celtic had gone nine games without a victory over their Old Firm rivals, but they blasted that hoodoo.

Stanton was immense in the rearguard that came in for a second-half pounding after Joe Craig had put Celtic ahead with an absolutely unstoppable effort from 20 yards.

While Stanton calmed down things at the back Aitken worked non-stop in the middle of the park. In fact, it was the powerful Aitken who helped set up the only goal of the game when he surged through from a pass by Ronnie Glavin. He shaped to go right and then slipped the ball to Craig on the left. He kept on running for the return and the Rangers defence was caught out when Craig decided to go it alone.

Aitken is quiet and sensible and

Who is Celtic's star of the future?

ROY'S THE BOY!

THE youngster had tears in his eyes. His determined hopes of a Cup medal had vanished with the final whistle. He stood on the pitch, the picture of utter dejection, as the rival captain went up to collect the trophy, the winner's prize.

Celtic manager Jock Stein went over to him and said quietly: "You were the best man on the pitch. No doubt about it."

The boy on the receiving end of that compliment was Roy Aitken, the versatile Parkhead star who is now being likened to the late, great Duncan Edwards, of Manchester United.

It was after this season's League Cup Final at Hampden that Aitken had looked so sad. He had given everything he had, ran all day, but the Cup still went to Aberdeen when Davie Robb scored the winning goal in extra-time.

Stein's words were not rash. Many critics also acclaimed Aitken as the man of the match and that is praise indeed when you consider there were the likes of Danny McGrain, Kenny Dalglish, Joe Harper and Arthur Graham on the pitch that day.

Aitken was spotted by Stein while playing for Celtic Boys' Club only two years ago. The Parkhead supremo said then the boy would be a regular in the Celtic first-team within two years.

Aitken has kept his early promise and proved Stein absolutely accurate. He made the first-team break-

Pat Stanton (above) has had a big influence on the Celtic defence.

through last season as a centre-half, but this season he has moved to a new role on the left-hand side of the midfield.

The 18-year-old has looked every inch a star of the future. He could be as big a name as any that has come off the Parkhead conveyor belt of talent and that includes Bobby Murdoch, Jimmy Johnstone, Tommy Gemmell, Kenny Dalglish and Danny McGrain.

One player who has done more than most to bring on Aitken on the park is former Hibs skipper Pat Stanton, who has fitted snugly into Celtic's back four. His calm assurance has made centre half Roddy MacDonald a far more effective player and his confidence has allowed Aitken freedom in the middle of the park.

"Roy will be a tremendous player," predicts Pat. "He is so sensible and although he is only 18 he has a maturity rare in one so young. He is a real 100 per cent man and it's a pleasure to play beside him.

"As for myself, I am just delighted to be at Parkhead I had no thoughts of a move from Hibs, but going to Celtic has given me a fresh motivation. They really are a great club with so many talented players."

The influence of Stanton was clearly shown in the Old Firm match against Rangers at Ibrox this sea-

refuses to accept any tag of "wonderboy". He stresses: "I've a lot to do yet. I know that. I'm just happy to be in the first-team.

"My best position? I'll play anywhere Mr Stein tells me to. He's the boss, after all. He makes the decisions and the players carry them out to the best of their ability."

Another player who can take great credit for the progress of Aitken is Bobby Lennox, the oldest player at Parkhead. Unfortunately, Bobby broke an ankle in that match against Rangers.

Bobby, the last of Celtic's European Cup-winning side of '67, stays close to Aitken in Ayrshire and they get together sometimes to train and to talk about the game.

Stein says: "Bobby and Roy are forever talking about football. It's good to see such enthusiasm."

Roy Aitken may be a boy in a man's game, but his determination and overall ability will certainly put years on rival teams!

HOPES and FEARS for 1978

INTERNATIONAL

England

RON GREENWOOD

"**I** HAVE always wanted to be part and parcel of a successful England set-up and it is my dearest wish that we should build a side capable of winning the European Championship in Rome in 1980 and the World Cup in Spain in 1982.

"When West Ham won the European Cup-Winners' Cup in 1965 and England the World Cup a year later. I remember bursting with pride for this country and the sort of football we produced to beat the rest of the world.

"Unfortunately, we allowed defensive-minded people to get a grip on our game and for the past few years our spectators have expected this sort of football, while the rest of the Continent has been going forward in technique.

"I remember being at a F.I.F.A. meeting with Sir Stanley Rous, Helmut Schoen and Sir Alf Ramsey and most of Europe's top men when we were discussing possible changes in the laws to get over the problems of defensive football.

"My comment was we were talking rubbish because if we weren't creative enough to find ways of defeating negative thinking we shouldn't be in the game.

"I still believe that and I am thrilled clubs like Nottingham Forest, Everton, Coventry and Norwich are being successful with more adventurous football.

"If I had a wish on a wider front for 1978 it would be more clubs adopt this philosophy. I have never used

blackboard in my life and I hope more people will realise football is a sport to be enjoyed.

"If I have a fear for 1978 it is too many school-teachers get it into their heads they have to be filling boys' heads with systems, formations, styles of play, permeated by television.

"A New Year Resolution? To work hard at the job of England manager which is the top honour in football so people will say: 'He did a good job'."

●●●●●●●●●●

N. Ireland

DANNY BLANCHFLOWER

"*I* CONSIDER I have some reason for hope in 1978 — and it stems from my team's World Cup qualifying game against Belgium in Belfast in November.

"Before the match I told the players they had nothing to fear against Belgium. On paper, they had the players capable of beating us, but we went at them and it came off for us. And what was particularly satisfying for me was the performance of Gerry Armstrong.

"Now, I'm looking ahead to us being able to serve up similar football in 1978. My fear is the team, and Gerry Armstrong, may not be able to repeat their Belgium performance.

"Fortunately, Gerry has plenty of confidence. And against Belgium, also showed he had ability. It is too early to assess what sort of job I've done with Northern Ireland, but I'll continue to work as hard as I can."

Ron Greenwood was proud of West Ham's European Cup-Winners' Cup success in 1965.

Scotland

ALLY MacLEOD

"**S**COTLAND, World Cup winners 1978 . . . that's my hope and dream. We go to Argentina in June as Britain's only representative and we don't want to let anyone down.

"Can we win it? Of course we can! We will be going with confidence and I know my boys can do a good job out there. Let's face it, we must be a competent side to have beaten current European Champions Czechoslovakia and the improving Welsh side in our section.

"The last time Scotland reached the World Cup Finals was only four years ago in West Germany, but although we were unbeaten the Scots went home empty-handed. Obviously I want us to be unbeaten again, but this time I want something to show for our efforts.

"My fear? Just that Scotland are allowed to play some good football in Argentina. I don't want teams to prevent us showing our skills to the

world. Obviously they are not going to step back and allow us to destroy them, however, I hope the Finals are played in a sporting manner."

●●●●●●●●●●

Wales

MIKE SMITH

"*H*OPES must always be with players, especially those with the kind of exciting talent such as Brian Flynn and Joey Jones who, although they may seem established already, are still improving with every international.

"Then we have newly arrived players such as Les Tibbott, David Jones, Carl Harris and Donato Nardiello who share one common quality — they are in First Division football.

"Players like Harris, Nardiello, Nick Deacy with Eindhoven, Mickey Thomas and Alan Curtis are, suddenly, competing for the goalscoring positions against world class men like John Toshack and Leighton James.

"I've always envied countries like Czechoslovakia who made seven changes against us recently and still came up with a powerful side. Yet we are approaching that kind of strength ourselves now and I took it as a great compliment recently when their manager Vaclac Jezek said we were harder opposition to beat than England or Scotland.

"Fears? Not an emotion I believe in. I have never presented anything to players in those terms. There was a fear of losing when we played Yugoslavia in the Quarter-Finals of the last European Championship; we have put that right and now our football possesses a new dimension.

"Certainly there is no fear among the players for the games ahead: England, who will be seeking revenge after our defeat over them at Wembley, and Scotland just before their departure for the World Cup Finals.

"The same goes for our European Championship qualifying matches against an astonishing diversity of opponents: from the best team in the World, West Germany, to Turkey and Malta where climate and playing surfaces present special problems. But, these days, Wales fear no one."

●●●●●●●●●●●
Republic of Ireland
JOHNNY GILES

"**M**Y ONE fear for 1978 is we will get the same referee for our European Championship game in Bulgaria as we had for our World Cup tie there in June.

"I've particular reason for recalling that Sofia game for we had a seemingly good goal disallowed at a vital stage as the Republic went down 2-1 — and out of World Cup contention.

"My hopes for the coming year are twofold and straightforward. I'm hoping Shamrock Rovers will win the League of Ireland title for the first time since 1964 and the international team will get maximum points from our European Championship games.

"I think the trends in the game in Ireland are pretty good at the moment, but I would like to see more emphasis on constructive rather than destructive things at all levels of the game.

"My personal wish for the New Year is to be as content in 1978 as I was in 1977."

FOOTBALL LEAGUE
First Division
TERRY NEILL Arsenal

"**I** BELIEVE it wise to be positive without going overboard about winning this, that and the other.

"Arsenal have certainly improved. We have made progress, and although we still have work to do, my hope for 1978 is we continue to make the same progress.

"It is too early to make predictions. But it is nice to be in a position where people want your predictions.

"I want to give the Arsenal supporters joy and a lot of pleasure from watching us play. Not only through results but by the way we play. This is very important.

"We have done a lot of hard work. By 'we' I refer to the coaching staff, the players and the people behind the scenes at Highbury.

"Of course it would be tremendous to win a major honour. But it would be doubly nice if we won it playing entertaining football, the stuff that makes people glad they came to watch."

Second Division
LAWRIE McMENEMY Southampton

"**W**HAT do I want in 1978? That's easy — promotion for Southampton.

"Quite honestly I think you'd get the same answer from everyone at the Dell.

"Every manager will say the same thing, but I think it's more important for this club than almost any other in the country.

"In a lovely period for the club we won the F.A. Cup two years ago, and last season we had the thrill of playing in Europe while re-shaping the team.

"Now we have done that it is imperative we give our supporters the best football we can offer and that means getting back to the First Division.

"My fear is obvious. That Saints fail to make it this season. We have had a large clear-out, and of the team that won the Cup, only four are left, and only one, Nick Holmes, has been in the side recently.

"People will tell you this is the best Second Division for years, so it would mean even more to win it. Promotion would really put the candles on the cake. Everyone here is working towards that end, and I would love to go up for the sake of our chairman, the entire staff and our 20,000 regular and loyal supporters.

"As for a New Year Resolution, well I'm learning the longer you live in this game the more you want to preach enjoyment and put the emphasis on skills rather than results. I would like to increase my endeavours in this direction and try to influence other people to adopt the same philosophy."

Third Division
ARFON GRIFFITHS Wrexham

"**I**T'S AN easy answer. The hope is promotion; the fear is we let it slip again as we did last season. Everyone sees Wrexham's football in those straight-forward terms — and that's the way it is.

"I'm not going to start shouting about anything yet. Let's win something first. But, in terms of hope, we've a couple of things going for us. We're not letting in some easy goals as we did last season and the pressure may not be so intense.

"Last season we were winning games so consistently. So were Mansfield, Brighton and Crystal

Palace. Now those three clubs have gone and I don't think the competition is quite so fierce.

"Of course, there comes a time when the circumstances create their own pressure. This season, if we stay out in front, I believe we are better equipped to handle it.

"Now we have the experience of Dai Davies, Dixie McNeil and Les Cartwright. Also, when we lost promotion in the last five matches of last season, it was the first setback the younger players had known in their careers.

"They've come out of it as better professionals and as better men. So, while the fear of failure remains after the experience of last season, we have the right attitude, approach and players to conquer it."

Fourth Division
GRAHAM TAYLOR Watford

"**W**HEN I joined Watford during the summer I said we were not good enough to win promotion. But I was wrong. So much so promotion to the Third Division is our one and only aim.

"My mistake was I judged the squad I inherited by my own standards, the standards I demand. I did not judge them by the rest of the Fourth Division.

"Clearly we are good enough to win the Championship. But now we must guard against complacency. Because if we fail to go up we are considered failures. That is one of the cruel ironies of setting high standards from the beginning.

"My one problem centres around everyone else's belief we are certs. If Watford drop a home point people look at the result in disbelief and mutter about how quickly a top of the table lead can be whittled down!

"In 1978 I must ensure my squad are capable of playing as a top of the table team. Because that brings a type of pressure some of the lads have not experienced before."

Everybody works hard behind-the-scenes at Highbury.

Continued overleaf

SCOTLAND'S VALUE OF

ON WEDNESDAY, October 12th, 1977, when Scotland beat Wales to qualify for the 1978 World Cup Finals in Argentina, the transfer value of everyone in the Scotland squad was immediately enhanced.

Clubs who subsequently made enquiries about any of the international members were invariably told their value had soared since qualification.

SHOOT decided to take a look at 16 of the players likely to be included in Ally MacLeod's Argentina-bound squad, to assess their form this season for their clubs, and place uprated prices on their heads.

ALAN ROUGH (PARTICK)

26-year-old Rough has been on the transfer list for some time now without moving. We find it very hard to understand, especially as he is Scotland's number one goalkeeper and playing consistently well for his Premier Division club Partick Thistle.

Shoot Value: £100,000

SANDY JARDINE (RANGERS)

29-year-old Jardine is playing a vital part in helping his club to the Premier Division Championship with some sturdy performances in the Ibrox Park defence. A talented full-back who loves to over-lap and scores a fair share of goals from that position.

Shoot Value: £125,000

TOM FORSYTH (RANGERS)

Plays alongside Jardine in the defence for Rangers. He has been a model of consistency as their goals-against column indicates. The 29-year-old has gained in confidence over the past few years and has developed into a fine sweeper.

Shoot Value: £170,000

WILLIE DONACHIE (MAN. CITY)

As City search for honours, Donachie is playing a major role. No longer are they a soft touch away from home, and the 26-year-old full-back epitomises their new-found steel. Banned from the opening World Cup game because of two yellow cards in qualifying ties.

Shoot Value: £300,000

GORDON McQUEEN (LEEDS)

Regarded by many as the best centrehalf in Europe at present. This is true when you consider the number of clubs enquiring to buy the blond 25-year-old who is on the Elland Road transfer list. Powerful in the air and at set-pieces.

Shoot Value: £440,000

WILLIE DONACHIE

SUCCESS BOOSTS WORLD CUP STARS

LOU MACARI (MAN. UTD.)

As Manchester United struggle to find consistency, their 28-year-old little midfielder Macari, who scored Division One's first hat-trick this season, has been playing tremendously. Always in the thick of the action and gets his name on the scoresheet regularly.

Shoot Value: £350,000.

DON MASSON (DERBY)

A cultured midfield player who arrived late on the international front but who is operating superbly. Since moving to Derby earlier this season the 32-year-old Masson has been playing some of the best football of his career.

Shoot Value: £200,000

KENNY DALGLISH (LIVERPOOL)

Has fully justified the massive fee paid by Liverpool before the start of the season. The 26-year-old Dalglish is their top scorer, and his goals have helped 'Pool to the League Cup Semi-Finals and kept them in pursuit of Nottingham Forest in the First Division Championship race.

Shoot Value: £500,000

ASA HARTFORD (MAN. CITY)

Midfield inspiration of City and Scotland, Asa has played a leading part in the Maine Road club's fine season so far. World Cup observers in Argentina will admire the 27-year-old's tremendous work-rate for Scotland. Leeds must be kicking themselves for calling off a £170,000 transfer back in November, 1971.

Shoot Value: £350,000.

JOE JORDAN (MAN. UTD.)

Despite the critics who say striker Joe is not a consistent goalscorer Manchester United's massive £350,000 signing of Joe will prove money well spent. The 26-year-old Scot is one of the most fearless players in the game and his non-stop worrying upsets the best of defences.

Shoot Value: £350,000

WILLIE JOHNSTON (W.B.A.)

Scotland will be hoping their 31-year-old winger will keep out of trouble in Argentina. His quick temper has seen him sent-off ten times in his career. But his brilliant ball-control and accurate centres makes him a must for the well-balanced side Scotland take to Argentina where they will value his whole-hearted displays.

Shoot Value: £160,000

MARTIN BUCHAN (MAN. UTD.)

28-year-old Martin is a brilliant defender, very cool under pressure and quick to see a chance to break from defence and set his team or country on the attack. He has skippered Scotland and is the inspiring captain of the Old Traffold club and as such led them to their F.A. Cup triumph in May.

Shoot Value: £320,000.

BRUCE RIOCH (DERBY)

Hard-tackling midfielder who has already been featured in three big transfer deals. The 30-year-old's tremendous shooting has seen him score many spectacular goals for club and country. Bruce once scored four goals in a match v Tottenham when tried as a central striker in his first spell with Derby.

Shoot Value: £200,000

ANDY GRAY (ASTON VILLA)

Central striker Andy is only 22 and is already one of the most feared strikers in the world. Brilliant in the air and is on the half chance in a flash. He missed three of Scotland's World Cup qualifying games after being sent-off v the Czechs. Is now free to lead the Scottish attack in the World Cup Finals.

Shoot Value: £450,000.

GEORGE WOOD (EVERTON)

Everton paid Blackpool £150,000 for George in August, 1977, and the brilliant displays of the Douglas-born 23-year-old have placed him well in the running for the number two goal-keeper spot in Scotland's World Cup squad when it is named by boss Ally MacLeod. Very agile and has quick reflexes.

Shoot Value: £200,000

DANNY McGRAIN (CELTIC)

Celtic and Scotland supporters will be hoping 27-year-old Danny will soon be back in action. Rated by many experts the best full-back in the world, Danny is an automatic choice for his country. Celtic's low League position is proof of how much he has been missed by his club.

Shoot Value: £300,000

ANDY GRAY

GEORGE WOOD

ASA HARTFORD

MARTIN BUCHAN

WILLIE JOHNSTON

KENNY DALGLISH

DON MASSON

THE FRANCIS DEBATE

'LET FRANCIS PLAY IN AMERICA'

Says Arsenal's LIAM BRADY

WHEN Britain is trying to achieve economic stability, it seems ridiculous that a transfer fee of one million pounds should be paid out for a player. But having said that, I wish the player concerned, Trevor Francis, all the luck in the world. The former Birmingham City striker has all the skills necessary for success. In past years, he has been with a club who have not managed to win any of the major trophies, and can't be blamed for joining one which is actively concerned in League and Cup competitions.

About controversy surrounding the fact that Trevor has won permission to play summer football in the United States, it is difficult for me to judge whether or not this is a good thing, because I've never experienced soccer over there. But on the face of it, I can't see any harm in spending the close season in America. There doesn't appear to be a lot of stress playing in that class of football, and in the sunshine.

Though there must be pressure on any player who breaks the price barrier of £1m, the publicity surrounding the move, the money paid out, all help to put the player in a position in which he is keenly conscious of what is expected of him. In the case of a £400,000 price tag, I don't believe that a player transferred for that figure today feels the earth has been paid for him. That sum is becoming more commonplace every day. There is no need for a player to feel under pressure in these circumstances.

Obtaining Freedom of Contract is one way in which players have moved in an attempt to bring about a change in the transfer system. However, there can be a snag in a player holding a four-year contract — he may be unhappy at a club in the middle of it, say two years, then someone is liable to step in and buy him.

Summing-up, a £1m transfer fee seems unreal even in these times of inflation, but at the moment, we are stuck with it.

'FOREST WILL GET THEIR MONEY BACK'

Says Bristol City's JOE ROYLE

IT'S the law of supply and demand that creates the £1m transfer, and the actual price paid for a player should not necessarily be a measure of his ability. For example, it shouldn't follow that a man who costs a club £1m is ten times better than someone who has been transferred for £100,000.

In the case of Trevor Francis, however, I think it best to take a positive outlook, and consider the good things that have come out of his transfer. First, both clubs concerned with his move are happy. Birmingham have cleared off their overdraft, and Nottingham Forest have secured the star striker they wanted. Second, the money is kept in the game, and third, Trevor is satisfied.

Of course, the transfer fee itself is a manufactured one, and I don't know just how it is decided upon by the managers. Certainly, the player himself has nothing to do with it. But I would say that Forest will get their money back if they can win a couple of trophies during the next three seasons, and at the end of that time they can still expect to have Francis on their books.

And on the subject of how the amount of a transfer fee is decided, it is worth noting that a fee of £750,000 has been mentioned in connection with England B striker Mike Flanagan, a striker who is not even in the First Division!

One unusual factor in the transfer of Trevor Francis lies in the fact that none of the accepted big-money clubs, such as Everton, Liverpool, the two Manchester clubs, or Arsenal, were involved. The two clubs most interested in the player were Coventry and Nottingham Forest.

Through the years, transfer fees have rocketed with inflation, and fees which caused a sensation in the Sixties wouldn't flutter an eyelash today. Sadly, the sum of money involved doesn't always guarantee the man concerned will be a success with his new club. Take Derek Hales for instance. He hardly hit it off at Derby.

One factor in the deal is guaranteed. The crowds will flock to see the first £1m man. In Trevor Francis, Nottingham Forest have bought a player who is a credit to the game, and a nice fellow as well. As I said before, his move should benefit all concerned.

CONTINUES...

Football League managers have had their say about Brian Clough's decision to splash-out £1 million on Trevor Francis.

'Joe Public' has also made a meal of the Birmingham-Forest transfer coup, finding it welcome relief from the political unrest and industrial strife that has gripped the country this winter.

Now, the players themselves discuss one of the most sensational transfers in football history in a special SHOOT forum . . .

'ABOLISH THE TRANSFER SYSTEM'

Says Ipswich's CLIVE WOODS

ONE obvious effect the £1m transfer of Trevor Francis could have is to boost an already inflationary transfer market. A reserve team player, for instance, who would have been worth £50,000 before the Birmingham-Forest deal could find his value boosted to £200,000. But in spite of this, I can't see the £1m transfer being repeated, or a player being transferred in this country for a higher amount — for a few seasons at least.

Where are the players who could command such a sum? Only a small, select band could possibly come into this category.

I would like to see the transfer system, as we know it, abolished. I don't know what the solution is, but if club managers, Football League and Football Association officials get together they might find a way to improve on the present situation. As it is, clubs like Norwich, Bristol City and Ipswich have no way of competing for high-priced players. Only Liverpool, Everton, Manchester United, Manchester City, Arsenal and Leeds can afford high fees, yet even they would think twice before paying out a sum of £1m.

Nottingham Forest, an ambitious club determined to gain success in League and Cup competitions, have not been scoring freely this season and obviously calculated that Trevor Francis was the type of striker they needed.

But buying in a big way is no guarantee of success, and as a player expected to supply the goals, a certain burden is placed on Trevor's shoulders. Of course, his record proves he is a goalscorer, and players of his class are rare. Yet to make good on the amount of money they have laid out, Forest must start winning trophies in the immediate future.

As League Champions and big spenders, Forest have staked their claim for inclusion in that select group of elite clubs. Yet it keeps coming back to me that £1m is an unbelievable sum to spend on one player. It wouldn't worry me if such a transfer deal is never repeated in Britain. The transfer system has gone mad.

BRIAN Clough and Peter Taylor, both astute men, would not think of spending £1m on a player unless they thought he was worth it. In capturing Trevor Francis they have bought a striker who maintains a high scoring average season after season. He is young, and with luck could give Nottingham Forest at least another ten years' service.

In a big-money deal of this sort, I believe the matter of whether or not it is a good or bad thing is really related to the two clubs concerned, and the player. If they are satisfied, then there is justification

'BRUM'S FAILURES COST FRANCIS HONOURS'

Says West Brom's TONY BROWN

for such a transfer.

Admittedly, Birmingham may not be happy at losing a player of the calibre of Trevor Francis, because money isn't everything and it will be difficult to replace him. But the club looks doomed to Second Division football anyway, and the money they have secured from the transfer can go on buying a couple of players to help them secure promotion should they go down.

Even with Trevor in the line up during the last few seasons, Birmingham have been struggling to make a name for themselves, which must have cost Francis a fair number of international caps had he been with a more successful club.

Naturally, the £1m fee paid out by Nottingham Forest captured all the sporting headlines and the imagination of the fans, whether they approved of it or not. Now that this record-breaking transfer has become a reality, the chances are that similar deals could follow in the future.

Like any player, Trevor is anxious to get among the honours, and if Forest continue to be successful, he can't expect to be turning out in 60 or 70 matches a season, which highlights the question of him playing in America during the close season. I see nothing wrong in this, but feel that after an arduous season in Britain involving a heavy playing schedule, Trevor himself may consider he is ready for a rest.

Francis celebrates a goal for Detroit Express.

AFTER missing so many games during 1978, I didn't believe things could get any worse. I was wrong. Two days before I was scheduled to make my comeback for Aston Villa against Nottingham Forest, I was training and slipped in the mud.

I was twisting and turning . . . and as I fell I twisted my knee. I realised right away that I'd torn a cartilage; perhaps I had torn it very slightly against Luton Town in the League Cup, when I damaged ankle ligaments, but I was feeling really good in training until that injury.

I had a cartilage operation — on the same right knee — as a Dundee United player and wasn't surprised when the club specialist told me an operation was necessary.

I was sick. I'd worked so hard to get fit, going through what was almost a second pre-season stint. I've played just 12 games this season and was itching to get back into action.

Instead, I entered hospital on the Wednesday for my operation.

At 6.30 a.m. on the Thursday morning I was woken up — I thought there must have been a fire! Half past six in the morning! I had tea and toast at seven and was allowed nothing more to eat or drink before my op at two o'clock.

I was very worried. Cartilage operations are painful and even if you can make a relatively quick recovery, initially your knee feels like a bus has run over it!

What if something went wrong? What if my run of bad luck got worse? Many things went through my mind that morning.

At one o'clock I was given the pre-op injection, which makes you very dry. Forty-five minutes later I was wheeled to the operating theatre and I remember signing autographs for doctors and nurses a few minutes before I went "out"!

I was given another injection and counted eight seconds on the clock before it took effect. The next I knew it was 11 p.m., and my leg felt like a balloon.

I had a drip attached to the knee and if there's one thing worse than

the sight of blood, it's the sight of your own blood! I was feeling pretty low, in some pain, but as I'd just come out of the anaesthetic I couldn't have a sleeping pill. My leg was so sore I didn't, in fact, sleep until Friday night.

On the Friday morning I began lifting the leg — the road to recovery couldn't begin early enough. A few of the lads popped in to visit me, and that certainly raised my spirits.

I asked if I could go home the next day and was discharged on the

(Left) "Injured against Luton Town in the League Cup."
(Right) "On crutches after taking a tumble against Everton a year ago."

glowing terms, it can't help but give you a boost.

My luck must surely change. I've got over the depression and now all I want to do is to get back into action. I miss the day-to-day involvement of full-time training, and as the world's worst spectator I don't go to see the lads play.

Bad patch

It used to hurt me when people said I was injury prone. Now, it goes in one ear and out the other. In fact, it's become rather boring. I feel I'm just going through a bad patch. The same has been said of other players and they've bounced back, which is exactly what I mean to do.

Perhaps the most disappointing aspect, for me, personally, has been that I've had to miss Scotland's game against Belgium. Regular

seat, having won in Austria.

Scotland badly need a good result and performance to give us something to build on. Although we beat Norway 3-2, the performance was hardly convincing and we were a little fortunate to scrape home 3-2.

Jock Stein has been quoted as saying that "too many of the players are used to losing" and changes may be on the cards.

Worrying

I doubt whether we'll see too many, but he obviously has the 1982 World Cup in mind and will want to build his side before then.

The most worrying aspect is our away form. I forget the last time we won away from Hampden, and I don't count matches against the other British sides as "away" victories.

The fans and Press are becoming disillusioned and it's up to the team to raise everyone's confidence again.

Join me again in a fortnight.

'TOO MANY INJURIES –BUT I SHAN'T CHANGE MY STYLE'

Saturday.

As I write, I have no date fixed for a return. I'm impatient, but there is no way I'm going to rush and risk more damage.

Having had a cartilage operation before, I know pretty well what to do and what progress I ought to be making. I'm happy with the way things are going and I'm hoping to be back sometime next month, but I'll think about that nearer the date.

Despite this latest set-back, I stand by what I said in SHOOT recently: that I shan't be changing my style. All I've ever achieved has been accomplished by going in where it hurts. I can't see myself altering.

Dived in

The tackle that started it all was against Luton, a 70-30 ball in favour of the Luton defender. I suppose I should have let him clear it . . . but you know me! Maybe it was stupid. I dived in and, well, you know the rest.

I can't say that I'd never do it again. No player can ever say he definitely won't do this or that. With 40,000 fans roaring you on, you do things on the spur of the moment and I know I'll be as competitive as ever.

It was good to hear Brian Clough praising me on television, saying it was bravery that had caused my injuries. When someone like Brian Clough talks about you in such

SHOOT readers will know how upset I was to miss out on the World Cup Finals. I've fought so hard to get back into the international reckoning and after playing against Austria and Norway this season I had hoped to make the number nine shirt my own.

I hope Jock Stein won't forget me. I doubt if he will, he's not that sort of manager. I should get quite a few games under my belt before the British Championship comes round in May, so my fingers are crossed.

In the meantime, Scotland take on Belgium, at Hampden Park, next week in a game we simply can't afford to even draw, let alone lose. Group Two is still very wide open, even if Portugal are in the driving

(Right) "Kenny Dalglish shoots but Scotland lost 3-2 in Austria."

FOCUS ON

GARRY BIRTLES
NOTTINGHAM FOREST

FULL NAME: Garry Birtles
BIRTHPLACE: Nottingham
BIRTHDATE: 27th June, 1956
HEIGHT: 6ft 1in
WEIGHT: 11st 6lbs
PREVIOUS CLUBS: None
MARRIED: Yes to Sandra
CHILDREN: No
CAR: Capri 2000
FAVOURITE PLAYER: Former Manchester United star, George Best
FAVOURITE OTHER TEAM: Manchester United
MOST DIFFICULT OPPONENT: Bristol City defender, Norman Hunter
MOST MEMORABLE MATCH: Beating Liverpool in the first-leg of this season's European Cup
BIGGEST THRILL: Being picked for my

First Division debut
BIGGEST DISAPPOINTMENT: Being turned down by Aston Villa at the age of 15
BEST COUNTRY VISITED: Austria
FAVOURITE FOOD: Steak
MISCELLANEOUS LIKES: Squash and good friends
MISCELLANEOUS DISLIKES: Losing and false people
FAVOURITE T.V. SHOWS: Monty Python's Flying Circus and any programme which stars Leonard Rossiter
FAVOURITE SINGERS: Alice Cooper, David Bowie and Bryan Ferry
FAVOURITE ACTOR/ACTRESS: Clint Eastwood and Susan George
BEST FRIEND: Digby, my Pyrenean Mountain Dog
BIGGEST INFLUENCE ON CAREER: My wife and family, Geoff Barrowcliff and

Long Eaton Rovers
BIGGEST DRAG IN SOCCER: When I'm not scoring goals
INTERNATIONAL HONOURS: None yet
PERSONAL AMBITION: To be happy and honest in everything I do
PROFESSIONAL AMBITION: To keep scoring goals for Nottingham Forest
IF YOU WEREN'T A FOOTBALLER, WHAT DO YOU THINK YOU'D BE? A floor layer, my profession before I joined Forest
WHICH PERSON IN THE WORLD WOULD YOU MOST LIKE TO MEET? Pop star Alice Cooper or tennis player Jimmy Connors

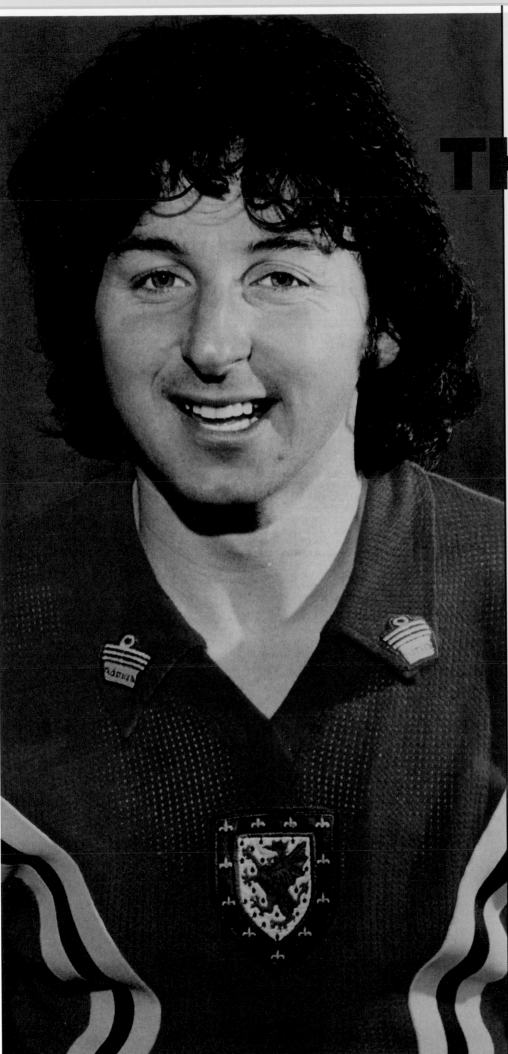

FOCUS ON
MIKE THOMAS
Manchester Utd. and Wales

FULL NAME: Michael Thomas
BIRTHPLACE: Mochdre, Colwyn Bay
BIRTHDATE: 7th July, 1954
HEIGHT: 5ft 6ins
WEIGHT: 10st 4lbs
PREVIOUS CLUBS: Wrexham
MARRIED: No, but I'm open to offers
CAR: Rover 2600
FAVOURITE PLAYER: Wrexham's Les Cartwright
FAVOURITE OTHER TEAM: Wrexham and Mountain View (Mochdre)
MOST DIFFICULT OPPONENT: Arsenal's Pat Rice
MOST MEMORABLE MATCH: Being captain of the Welsh Under-21 team against Scotland
BIGGEST THRILL: Signing for Manchester United
BIGGEST DISAPPOINTMENT: Every time we lose a match
BEST COUNTRY VISITED: Germany
FAVOURITE FOOD: Cornflakes and steak
MISCELLANEOUS LIKES: Going for long walks along the beach at Colwyn Bay
MISCELLANEOUS DISLIKES: People that moan
FAVOURITE T.V. SHOWS: Jim'll Fix It and any sports programmes
FAVOURITE SINGERS: Rod Stewart and Barry White
FAVOURITE ACTOR/ACTRESS: Clint Eastwood and Barbra Streisand
BEST FRIENDS: Joey Jones, John Lyons and Les Cartwright at Wrexham
BIGGEST INFLUENCE ON CAREER: John Neal, Mike Smith, my father and mother and Richard Dodd my PE teacher
BIGGEST DRAG IN SOCCER: Hangers-on
INTERNATIONAL HONOURS: Youth, Under-21, Under-23 and full caps for Wales
PERSONAL AMBITION: To play in the First Division for the rest of my career
PROFESSIONAL AMBITION: I achieved it this season helping United reach the F.A. Cup Final
IF YOU WEREN'T A FOOTBALLER, WHAT DO YOU THINK YOU'D BE? Very unhappy
WHICH PERSON IN THE WORLD WOULD YOU MOST LIKE TO MEET? Television newsreader Anna Ford

'I'm too old

IN terms of Press publicity, Brian Clough can claim more mileage than a London taxi. Rarely a day goes by without some brash deed or comment staring out from the back pages — or even the front pages. Even a brusque 'no comment' from Clough somehow gets reported. Now, with English football on its way back to prominence, foreign journalists are beginning to take an interest in the colourful and controversial character who led Forest to the European Cup. Our friends from French magazine ONZE recently sent a man to interview Cloughie, and the French reporter got a laugh from the Forest boss by explaining that in France the Nottingham supremo is as widely known as Robin Hood.

"I've never heard that one before, but I don't object to the comparison at all!"

With the ice broken, Clough went on to make some revealing and amusing statements . . .

Clough on the Germans "One of my sons is studying German — in case they try another invasion! You can never tell with the Germans. I'll tell you a story about our European Cup Semi-Final against Cologne last year. After the 3-3 draw in the first-leg, their manager Hennes Weisweiler was all smiles, posing for photos with his arms round me, saying I was the best. Then what happened after we'd beaten them 1-0 in the return leg in Cologne? He turned his back on me and shut himself in the dressing-room with his team. No handshakes or photos. No accolades. No smiles for the Press. Finished. That's typically German for you."

Clough on his departure from Derby "No comment. You'd better ask the Derby directors about that. Or ask Archie Gemmill why he followed me to Forest."
Clough on Leeds United "Just a lightning visit! 44 days to be precise. Jock Stein was only there 45 days before he left to take on the Scotland job. You've heard what? That I said Palermo in Sicily was meant to be the Mafia headquarters, but I reckoned it was the Leeds dressing rooms? I said that? Well, it's possible. I say many things and I'm supposed to have said so much more . . . "

Clough on club directors "That subject is finished. Let's not speak about it. It's finished."
Clough on Brighton "They were the only club who came in with an offer after the Derby affair. Things didn't go too well. Part of the trouble was I lived in Derby, and my kids even had problems with their mates at school. At one stage I even told Simon he wasn't to take anything with Brighton colours into the class. We still live in Derby now because I have never wanted my kids to have to change their schooling."
Clough on Politics "I'm a Socialist, and I have been since I was 20. Possibly I'm more socialist now than ever. You think it's a paradox to be a socialist and drive a Mercedes 280 SE and earn big money? Everyone's entitled to his opinion. But you've only got to open your eyes to find reinforcement for your beliefs."
Clough on Peter Taylor "He was the goalkeeper at Middlesbrough and I was the centre-forward. We've rarely been apart since. Jimmy Gordon was our coach up there, and he's still with us too. He's 64 now, but he takes care of the training sessions at Forest. Peter and I think along the same lines, though he's more actively involved in recruiting players. His latest coup was to snatch Gary Mills of Northampton from under the noses of Arsenal. Peter kidnapped him at the last moment! Garry Birtles was another of Peter's successes. I travelled to see him in action, and I wasn't convinced. Even when we had him on trial for a month he wasn't outstanding. But Peter insisted, and he came through in a big way."

Clough on breaking the £1,000,000 barrier "Don't blame me! I didn't fix the price. Birmingham City did that. We weren't the only bidders. Coventry were interested and it got almost like an auction. We won. That's all there is to it. What people don't realise is that I've also earned a lot of money for Forest. I signed Archie Gemmill from Derby for £25,000 in a swop deal with John Middleton and sold him to Birmingham for £160,000. Peter Withe cost us £20,000 and I sold him for £250,000. I signed Chris Woods for £10 and sold him to Q.P.R. for £250,000."

★ **1980** The year at a glance... DIVISION ONE WINNERS: **Liverpool** ★ FA CUP WINNERS: **West Ham**

Clough on discipline "I don't think I've ever fined Kenny Burns for foul play. I've given him a few lectures, that's for sure. And he's had to play in the reserves. But he was named Footballer of the Year in 1977/78 — that says something, doesn't it? No, it isn't true that I fined Trevor Francis £50 for an unauthorised interview."

Clough on communicating with his players "With Trevor Francis I talk exclusively about dollars. With the others I talk whatever language I think will get through to them."

Cologne boss Hennes Weisweiler (far left) and Forest assistant manager Peter Taylor (bottom left).

Kenny Burns in trouble at Spurs (above, left). Trevor Francis (left), Britain's first £1 million player. Clough has made a conscious effort to stamp out hooliganism (below).

Clough on his 'anti-hooligan' campaign "No one's going to give me any medals for that. It's nothing special. I've got three kids and I think all fathers must be anti-hooligans. That's the least they can do. It's their duty as parents."

Clough on 'fanatical' British fans "I don't mind fans supporting their team. Except when it's Liverpool or Everton! Or worse still, the Manchester clubs! There seems to be no way of communicating with some of them, and they're just completely and blindly intolerant. And I won't even mention the religious bigotry in Glasgow."

Clough on his future "If I leave Forest, I'll retire from football. You don't believe me? Then you're mistaken. Manager of England? Too late. I'm too old."

SUPPOSING . . . just supposing . . . every player in the Football League was put up for transfer. Which players would make up the most expensive team? Not of fees already paid, but fees that the clubs would demand — and pay — for the players. You could argue all night, and still disagree, but here's our choice of

PETER SHILTON

VIV ANDERSON

DAVID O'LEARY

RUSSELL OSMAN

KENNY SANSOM

GLENN HODDLE

BRYAN ROBSON

GORDON COWANS

TREVOR FRANCIS

FRANK STAPLETON

GARY SHAW

connection together at the back. Anderson can be devastating on the overlap and has scored some sensational goals that any striker would be proud of.

RUSSELL OSMAN

WE have no hesitation in selecting Osman as our centre-half; or to predict he'll be England's number five in the 1982 World Cup Finals (if they qualify). The 22-year-old Ipswich stopper is having a marvellous season and his partnership with Terry Butcher must be the best in the League. Indeed, it is possible that the Ipswich pair could team-up for England in the not too distant future. Commanding in the air, Osman reads the game like a veteran and for a big feller is surprisingly quick on the deck. Dave Watson has served England magnificently. Now, it's Osman's turn.

DAVID O'LEARY

A DIFFICULT choice, with Terry Butcher and Alan Hansen in contention, but the Arsenal defender oozes class. He makes everything seem so easy and always appears to have time, the hallmark of every great player. Injuries have restricted O'Leary's (below) appearances this season, but there can be no doubt that apart from possibly Franz Beckenbauer and Ruud Krol, the Republic of Ireland star is the most accomplished sweeper in Europe.

PETER SHILTON

IT'S a sad comment, but the fact is there is a dearth of young goalkeeping talent. Even the great Gordon Banks can't see a ready replacement for Ray Clemence and Peter Shilton (left) in the England team. John Lukic and Gary Bailey are fighting to maintain the progress they showed a couple of years ago. Ron Greenwood even turned to the untried, inexperienced Perry Digweed, just signed by Brighton from Fulham's reserves, for a recent Under-21 squad. Goalkeepers have longer careers than outfield players. Look at the value Arsenal have had from Pat Jennings. With this in mind, we feel someone, somewhere would still be prepared to pay £500,000 for Peter Shilton — but they probably wouldn't for any of the younger 'keepers.

VIV ANDERSON

NOT too many right-backs around. Viv Anderson got the nod over Spurs' Chris Hughton by a whisker, although both are from the same attacking mould. The Forest star became the first black player to win a full England cap and if he hasn't established himself at that level yet, it's because Ron Greenwood has preferred to keep the Liverpool

MONEY COULDN'T BUY

KENNY SANSOM

HE was valued at £1 million earlier this season and since his transfer from Crystal Palace, Sansom has become an even better player. Derek Statham and Arthur Albiston are also valuable young left-backs, but Sansom must be the pick. In the European Championship Finals last summer he was the best left-back on view and bar injuries should hold his position in the England team for ten years. He's as strong as an ox, incredibly fast and good in the air, despite a lack of inches.

GLENN HODDLE

COULD be leaving Spurs for the Continent at the end of the season; if he does, it'll be interesting to see if he is appreciated even more in West Germany or Italy. Glenn (above) has all the skill and, for a midfielder, weighs in with his share of goals. There are those who still doubt his overall contribution, saying he fades during matches. Perhaps the slower pace of the Continental game will make Hoddle into the international star he is at present struggling to be.

BRYAN ROBSON

HIS West Brom manager has no doubt that Robson's best role is in midfield, although he could find himself playing in the back-four for England. Robson (above) is a modern day Paul Madeley, the type of player every manager dreams of, effective in several positions. His emergence in the England team will make it hard for Ray Wilkins to reclaim his anchor-man job in England's midfield, and Robson, although he doesn't have Wilkins' finesse, scores more goals than the Manchester United man.

GORDON COWANS

HE admitted recently that his form for Villa has been disappointing, but it's only a temporary lapse as Cowans is one of the most exciting young midfielders around. The greyhound-owning star has all the qualities of a midfield man: he can win the ball, use it intelligently and can score goals. He gets through a tremendous amount of work and is not afraid to try the unexpected. Andy Gray has constantly praised Cowans in his column and if Gordon continues to work hard at his game there is no reason why he shouldn't progress into the full England team.

TREVOR FRANCIS

NOT too long ago there were question marks over Francis' career. The Achilles tendon has healed perfectly and if anything the Forest star is an even better player than he was a year ago. No forward in England has the blistering pace of the England striker; he was our first £1 million player and Brian Clough would make a few bob should he ever sell Francis.

FRANK STAPLETON

WHAT! No Kenny Dalglish? While the Liverpool superstar is the most valued forward in Britain, at 30 he simply can't command the highest transfer fee. Stapleton is six years his junior and it's a fact of soccer life that youth will always cost more than experience. Stapleton has scored regularly since he became an Arsenal regular, whether he's been alongside John Radford, Malcolm Macdonald or Alan Sunderland. Don Howe thinks he's the best in Europe — and that's where he may be going at the end of the season.

GARY SHAW

FAVOURITE to be named Young Player of the Year by his fellow professionals this Sunday, the Aston Villa striker will also be favourite for SHOOT's Most Exciting Player of the Year award in a few weeks. Such has been his impact this season that he could well add full international honours to the England Under-21 cap he already has. Shaw is the type of player to pull in the fans. Quick, alert, brave, he tries things others don't even think about. When you see Villa and Shaw at their best, you wonder why the League chairmen needed to alter the rules to improve the game.

Trevor Francis takes on Arsenal's Pat Jennings.

I'VE never wanted anything more badly than to be handed England's number four shirt for next Tuesday's match against Northern Ireland at Wembley.

It's the boost I need after going through the most agonising, frustrating stage in my career following an injury in the League Cup Fifth Round replay against Barnsley.

While the leg wound healed I've had to watch Liverpool recover from a bad start and put together a string of great results that's put egg on the faces of the critics who'd written my club off.

Being included in the England team will lift my spirits sky high. I've never yet let my country down and all I ask is for the chance to prove my worth again.

I promise Ron Greenwood he won't regret it if he gives me the nod. In return, I'll give England everything I've got.

Missing so many games in Liverpool's tremendous winning run has obviously put a question mark against me. Dare Ron pick a man who lacks the week-in, week-out involvement of preparing for, and playing in, games at the highest level?

I might have lost that vital "edge", the split-second thinking and speed off the mark that separates an international from the bread and butter First Division player.

To wipe out any doubts in his mind I'm putting an extra-special effort into my training with the England squad. There's no one — not even Kevin Keegan himself — who's running harder, tackling harder, or listening harder to Ron Greenwood's tactical talks.

A lot of people parallel my situation with that of Dave Watson's before the final qualifying make-or-break game against Hungary at Wembley, which we won 1-0.

Then there was speculation about whether Ron would pick even a former regular like Dave, who was out of first team football and in Southampton reserves.

Instead, Ron chose West Ham's Alvin Martin, who justified the boss' faith in him. Whether Dave would have done as well, worse, or better, will never be known, of course.

But I don't see myself in the same fix as Dave. I have two things in my favour: I'm younger and could be back in the Liverpool team for the final stages of the season at least and helping to carry off silverware.

Already I'm banging on manager Bob Paisley's door, reminding him I'm ready, willing and able.

I'm sure Ron will want to pick players wearing that ring of confidence which comes from winning honours.

There's no point in England going to the World Cup Finals without the will to win the trophy. We must forget about our struggle to qualify and concentrate on moulding a

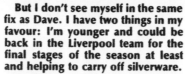

PHIL THOMPSON
My soccer world

team on a par with Liverpool.

We know we don't possess the brilliant superstars of countries such as Brazil and Argentina, players who have the ability to virtually win matches single-handed.

At present there are four "run-up" matches scheduled in which the emphasis will be on creating an eleven-man unit capable of doing the country proud on the plains of Spain, starting with Northern Ireland, our first opponents in this season's British Championship.

The Irish team are an example for England to follow. A fine mix of good professionals who slot together like pieces in a jigsaw.

Manager Billy Bingham has done wonders with a limited number of players — mainly from the English League — to choose from. Two years ago he took them to their first outright British Championship win since 1914, and now a place in the World Cup Finals after a gap of 24 years.

Like Scotland, they play with a lot of pride and passion, and we're in for a hard time at Wembley.

As usual, I expect it to be more like a League derby game than an

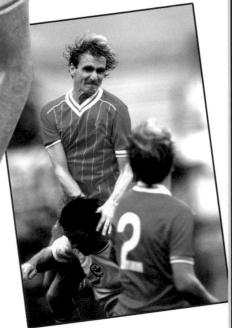

international, as so many of the players are familiar with each other's styles.

Unfortunately I haven't the space to go through their team, player by player, but I must mention Pat Jennings, who is not only a fantastic 'keeper but also one of the game's real gentlemen.

His honesty showed itself recently when he blamed himself for the rare mistake that let in the Spurs goal that knocked Arsenal out of the F.A. Cup.

With Pat at one end, and probably Ray Clemence at the other, and the outfielders playing "tight", there won't be many goals scored. I'd predict a 1-0 win — to England!

And I want to be part of it!

PICK ME -YOU WON'T REGRET IT, RON

HANS-PETER BRIEGEL

WEST GERMANY

A SUPERB 6ft. 2in., 14-stone athlete, Hans-Peter Briegel was outstanding in midfield as West Germany powered to their European Championship win in 1980, and showed that it was no fluke by overshadowing Diego Maradona in the Mundialito clash in Uruguay six months later.

Son of a German farmer, Briegel won ten youth titles as a decathlon competitor, and covered the 100 metres in 10.9 seconds. Soccer was just a hobby with local sides SV and TV Rodenbach until he joined 1.FC Kaiserlautern in 1975, rapidly becoming a regular first teamer in the centre of the defence.

Jupp Derwall called him into the national squad in 1979 and astutely used him to provide muscle and man-to-man marking in midfield — a job he does with verve and aggression before counter-attacking with breathtaking runs from the back.

With fewer than 30 caps to his credit, Briegel is still a relative newcomer to the international scene, but at 26 (birthdate October 11th, 1955) he's got ample time at the top to increase his score.

World Cup stars to watch

OSVALDO ARDILES

ARGENTINA

ARGENTINE manager Cesar Menotti says: "Ardiles was one of the key players in our 1978 victory. He's a world-class player because he produces good football, match after match, in all sectors of the pitch.

"He's fast mentally and physically, and even though some people say he's fragile, he isn't easy to bring down."

The Spurs midfielder is quick to admit that he was an ordinary player until he met Menotti in 1975 and began his international career.

It seemed unbelievable for the lawyer's son born in Cordoba on August 3rd, 1952, in the basketball-mad Juniors district.

Osvaldo joined Instituto at 13,

picked up four youth titles and, alongside Mario Kempes, won the provincial Championship in 1972.

He went on loan to Belgrano in 1974, before joining Huracan a year later, but was a hotly disputed choice when he made the first of his 45 appearances in the national team.

Menotti defended his decision and Ardiles more than answered the criticisms in six World Cup games.

Since his £325,000 move to London, the rest of the Ardiles story is already written in the Tottenham history books.

He has influenced the British attitude to overseas footballers more than any other player.

The Spurs Revolution

IT'S been a hectic summer. My son Lee was born, I've been setting up a business and buying a new house. I didn't have time to really relax before reporting back to Tottenham for pre-season training.

As usual, manager Keith Burkinshaw and a few of the club's directors were at Cheshunt to welcome the players back.

Keith outlined Tottenham's hopes and ambitions for 1983-84, introduced us to the two new players Gary Stevens and Danny Thomas . . . and then told us to take the afternoon off!

It was all part of Tottenham's revolutionary new pre-season training plan. Instead of the usual tough slog back to full fitness, we were to train mornings only from 10.30-12.00 for the first week.

We took it easy, building up from walks around Cheshunt to jogging and then running. Our thighs were measured every morning to see how the new methods had affected muscles.

No five-a-sides were played that first week, nor the usual exercises. In fact, we never even saw a ball.

The plan was devised by Keith, his assistant Peter Shreeves and physiotherapist Mike Varney after a general chat with the players last season.

It was introduced to reduce the risk of injury. In previous years players had suffered strains and hamstrings as a result of the rigours of hard pre-season training that lasted all day, every day for three weeks or more.

When you think about it, this system makes sense. Building the body up gradually gives the muscles time to strengthen.

My pal Gordon Strachan was staying with me for a few days and

Up front with STEVE ARCHIBALD

said he wasn't particularly looking forward to pre-season training with Aberdeen.

They are going to a training camp in West Germany for a couple of weeks.

Training camps might be great for managers and coaches, but I'd hate it. Spending so much time away from your family isn't my ideal way of preparing for a long, tough season.

There were two notable absentees when Spurs reported back . . . Ray Clemence, who was still on a holiday cruise with his wife and family, and Ossie Ardiles.

Ossie had returned from the

Canary Islands that morning and was delayed at the airport. But it didn't stop him joining me on the golf course.

I'd taken advantage of Keith's surprise afternoon off and was about to start play when there was a whistle from the club house. It was Ossie. He had simply dumped his cases at home, found out where I was and collected his clubs.

At present I'm living next door to Ossie in Ricky Villa's old house while my new place is completed.

Recovered

Fortunately, Ossie has recovered from the broken shin that forced him to miss so much of last season.

Garry Brooke, seriously hurt in a car crash, is also fully fit. So is Micky Hazard, who reported back £100 heavier!

At the end of last season he was looking a bit chubby and took some stick from Garth Crooks, who bet him £100 he'd come back overweight.

Mick obviously worked extremely hard during the break and is in tremendous shape.

At the time of writing, captain Steve Perryman was still undecided about signing a new contract, but Eire international Chris Hughton is expected to stay.

As I said in my previous column, if Spurs can keep their stars we'll have the strongest, most experienced squad in the country.

All the best . . .

Steve Archibald

HUGHTON PUTS CAPS BEFORE CASH

TOTTENHAM'S Chris Hughton has put country before cash and insists international caps are ample reward for footballing talent.

Hughton spoke up following the long-running dispute about whether players should get paid

every time they turn out for national teams.

He says: "I think the honour of a call-up is definitely enough and that's all that good professionals want.

"As soon as payments are made it takes away the prestige. With the current financial state of football so unsteady, it may be necessary for clubs to take cash, but I'm not keen on the idea."

Delighted

The Republic of Ireland full-back adds that clubs should be delighted when their players receive international recognition and let them play at all times.

"Clubs should be able to spot a player's potential early on and admit they might have a future international and so be prepared to let him go.

"As soon as kids sign apprentice forms they set their sights on representing their country. It's football at the top level.

"Getting injured while playing for your country is just something clubs have to put up with. It's been happening for years and will go on happening.

"And I don't agree that clubs should be compensated for injuries suffered while on international duty."

Hughton admits that Eire's chances of making the European Championship Finals are slim and only a major upset will get them there.

"We need some freak results if we are to make it.

"Spain must rank as favourites after beating us 2-0. But I rate Holland. They are a strong, young team and are better than the Spanish."

WHAT a difference a year makes. This time 12 months ago Paul Walsh was preparing for another season in the Second Division with Charlton Athletic.

Today he is the subject of high-priced transfer talk, feared by First Division defenders and an England international striker.

Walsh, of the lightning turn instant control and lethal shot, emerged as one of the few successes from England's otherwise disastrous three-match tour of Australia.

Bobby Robson's squad, full of new faces and untried hopefuls, fumbled and stumbled through three unforgettable fiascos against opposition that would struggle to hold first team places in the Fourth Division.

Moral

A 0-0 draw and a 1-1 draw were hailed as moral victories by the Australians. Only once did England manage a win — and that was thanks to Walsh.

The 20-year-old striker gave his all in a bid to prove to manager Bobby Robson that he has the class to become part of England's European Championship campaign.

And his single goal in the second game in Australia saved a considerable number of blushes.

Walsh himself describes his 12 months as 'unforgettable!'

Luton signed him for £150,000

last July and he quickly impressed beginning with a sizzling hat-trick against Notts County.

"But if someone told me that I would experience so many highs and lows in one season I would not have believed them," he says.

"First the transfer and First Division football. Then to find that Luton's a striker's dream because they play attacking skilful football.

"And when I made the England Under-21 side I was absolutely thrilled.

"Mind you, I also saw the other side of the coin — when the goals dried up and we slipped down the table into the danger zone. Those were very worrying weeks."

Luton's ultimate survival had a lot to do with Walsh's quick adaptation to the pace and pressures of the First Division.

Already Walsh has been compared with Jimmy Greaves and West German goal-machine, Gerd Muller.

"Very flattering," says Walsh, "but hardly true. I have a lot to learn and a long way to go before I can make any such claim.

"But at least it proves that

WINNER WALSH

people have been impressed with the form I have shown so far.

"Bobby Robson made my year when he invited me to join the England squad for the British Championships. I didn't play, but I became accustomed to the whole set up — a great thrill.

"I was very proud to be asked to go on the tour of Australia. I knew it was a great opportunity to show what I could do.

"Scoring was a bonus, and for all the criticism, we did not lose a game and conceded only one goal.

"England tried a lot of new players and everybody knows that any team needs to be reasonably settled to really impress away from home.

"Now I only hope that what I did in Australia will enable me to stake a claim for a regular place. If not then I'll battle next season to achieve that personal target."

Not bad for 12 months work, but that's the wonder of Walsh.

Walsh closes in on Australia's Steve O'Connor during England's recent tour Down Under.

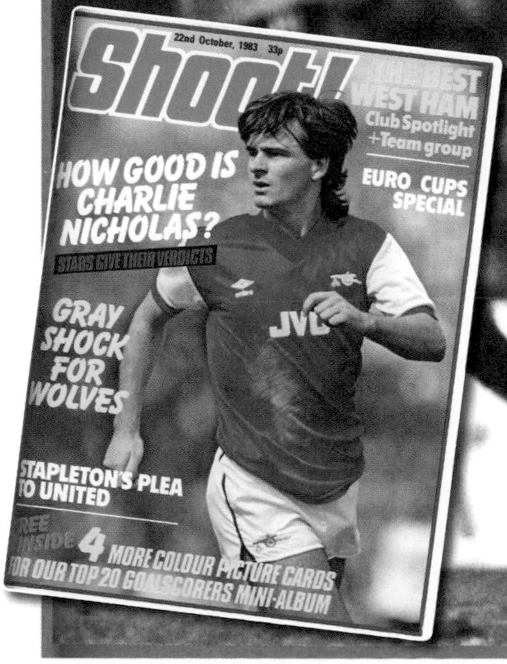

Why I've topped

KENNY DALGLISH

● He becomes the second post-War Liverpool player to score 100 goals in the League — Roger Hunt scored 160.

● 61 of his 100 have been scored at Anfield.

● He's scored two hat-tricks — both against Manchester City — and two times in 17 games. Ten of his 100 have been against Man. City and eight against Ipswich.

● He's also scored a club record 47 Cup goals, so his next milestone will be 150 in all — achieved by only two other Liverpool post-War players — Roger Hunt (285) and Billy Liddell (228).

I WAS staggered by the reaction to my 100th League goal for Liverpool!

Yes, I am very proud to become the first footballer to score a century of goals in both the Scottish League and the Football League. But from a professional point of view the most important thing about my goal at Ipswich was that it earned us an important point in our quest to retain the Championship.

While the statisticians were working out the figures, I was made very aware of something that nobody in the media, or indeed on the terraces, seemed to consider worthy of mention.

I believe that my record is proof, if proof was ever necessary, that I have had the good fortune to play for the most successful clubs in Britain.

When I was growing up with Celtic they were, without question, the best team in Scotland.

And when I joined Liverpool in 1977 they were, and still are, the best in England!

For once, Celtic aren't in the hoops. That's me in the dark shirt, taking on Morton's Davie Hayes before my transfer to Liverpool.

HIS SCOTTISH CENTURY

Opponents		1971-72 H	1971-72 A	1972-73 H	1972-73 A	1973-74 H	1973-74 A	1974-75 H	1974-75 A	1975-76 H	1975-76 A	1976-77 H	1976-77 A
Ayr United	(13)	—	1	—	2	—	1	1	—	1	3	2	—
Motherwell	(12)	—	2	1	2	—	—	1	—	2	2	2	1
Dundee	(10)	3	—	1	—	—	—	3	—	2	1	1	—
Hearts	(9)	—	1	—	—	2	2	—	—	2	—	1	1
Dundee Utd.	(8)	—	1	1	—	1	—	—	—	2	2	1	1
St. Johnstone	(8)	—	1	1	2	—	—	1	—	2	1	—	—
Clyde	(6)	1	1	—	—	1	1	1	1	—	—	—	—
Kilmarnock	(6)	2	—	—	2	—	—	1	1	—	—	—	—
Aberdeen	(6)	—	—	1	1	—	—	—	—	1	1	1	1ᵖ
Falkirk	(5)	1	—	—	2	1	1	—	—	—	—	—	—
Partick Th.	(5)	—	1	—	1	—	—	1	1	1	—	—	—
Hibernian	(5)	—	1	1	1	—	1	—	1	1	1ᵖ	—	—
Rangers	(4)	—	1	1	—	—	—	1	1	—	—	—	—
Dumbarton	(4)	—	—	1	—	1	1	1	1	—	—	—	—
Arbroath	(4)	—	—	1	—	1	—	1	1	—	—	—	—
East Fife	(3)	—	—	—	—	1	2	—	—	—	—	—	—
Airdrieonians	(2)	1	1	—	—	—	—	—	—	—	—	—	—
Dunfermline	(2)	—	—	—	—	2	—	—	—	—	—	—	—
		8	9	10	13	8	10	8	8	13	11	8¹ᵖ	6¹ᵖ
Goals	(112)	17		23		18		16		24		14²ᵖ	
*Games	(202)	31		32		33		33		35		35	

(*Incl. 3 games without scoring in 1970-71)

When top clubs sign you and play you it is all the evidence you need that you are doing well in your profession. And when the goals go in, you have to sit back and think carefully — weigh up your own contribution with that of all the players around you.

Without the support and service of the best players in the business I would never have come anywhere near the record I now hold.

Looking back I find that I recall certain goals immediately — not because they were spectacular but usually because of the actual game and its significance.

I remember my first League goal in a 'derby' game against Rangers. I scored it back in September, 1971, in front of 69,000 fans at Ibrox to help us to a memorable 3-2 win.

Here's my first goal in the Football League, scored on my Liverpool debut at Middlesbrough in 1977.

the ton twice

Rangers enjoyed a good first-half and were ahead when a left wing corner drifted to the far post. I cushioned it in my stomach and stuck it past Peter McCloy with my left foot.

I also remember my first goal against Rangers as Celtic's newly appointed captain in season '75-76.

It was on the opening day of the League season, again at Ibrox and another 69,000 crowd. I knocked a first-half chance past Peter McCloy — he's faced me many times — to give us the lead. But this time Rangers hit back to win 2-1. It was an omen because they went on to win the title!

Speaking of titles, I remember vividly the goal I scored at Falkirk on April 27, 1974. We'd enjoyed a magnificent season, going top in October, '73. But always there was Rangers, breathing down our necks, waiting for a slip-up.

David Hay, now manager at Celtic, found me in the box and after a tight run past two tackles I shot past Ally Donaldson. The game finished 1-1 ... and it was the game that clinched the Championship.

My first goal for Liverpool came at Ayresome Park, Middlesbrough.

Another one on the way to my ton, squeezing between Graham Moseley and Tony Grealish for a goal against Brighton last season.

But the goal that is always in my thoughts, when asked to recall one, is the first goal I scored at Anfield.

On an August evening, in front of more than 48,000 fans, I made the sort of home debut that players dream of. Ray Kennedy put me through on the inside left channel and I whipped a shot past Newcastle 'keeper Steve Hardwick ... in front of The Kop!

It's impossible to talk about goals for Liverpool and not recall some of my efforts against Everton.

And there is no way that I'll ever forget my first goal against The

Blues — why? Because it was the only one we scored against them that season and gave us a 1-1 draw at Anfield in March, 1979, after we'd lost 1-0 at Goodison earlier in the season.

Another goal against Everton sticks in my mind for a different reason ... it was a header!

Our game at Goodison in October, 1980, finished 2-2 and I notched a second-half equaliser by getting my head to a cross by Phil Neal. I celebrated in some style, but I doubt if Jim McDonagh in the Everton goal understood why.

And the day we beat them 3-1 at Anfield in November, 1981, brought me two goals against Everton for the first time.

The first came after Ronnie Whelan's powerful shot was beaten down by Jim Arnold. I pounced on the rebound. Terry McDermott put me through for the second which I steered wide of Jim.

But at the end of the day I must emphasise that football is, above all else, a team game. My goals are the product of 11 players, not one.

Kenny Dalglish

HIS ENGLISH CENTURY

Opponents		1977-78 H	A	1978-79 H	A	1979-80 H	A	1980-81 H	A	1981-82 H	A	1982-83 H	A	1983-84 H	A
Man. City	(10)	3	—	—	1	—	2	—	1	—	—	3	—	—	—
Ipswich	(8)	1	1	1	2	—	—	—	—	—	1	—	1	—	1
Aston Villa	(7)	—	2	1	—	—	—	—	2	—	—	—	1	1	—
Tottenham	(7)	—	—	—	2	—	—	—	—	1	2	2	—	—	—
W.B.A.	(5)	1	—	1	1	1	—	—	—	—	—	—	—	—	—
Bristol C.	(5)	1	—	—	1	1	2	—	—	—	—	—	—	—	—
Wolves	(5)	—	2	—	—	2	—	—	—	1	—	—	—	—	—
Brighton	(5)	—	—	—	—	—	—	—	2	—	—	1	2	—	—
Stoke	(5)	—	—	—	—	—	1	—	—	—	1	1	2	—	—
Derby	(4)	—	—	1	2	1	—	—	—	—	—	—	—	—	—
Everton	(4)	—	—	—	1	—	—	—	1	2	—	—	—	—	—
Arsenal	(4)	—	—	—	1	1	—	—	—	—	—	1	—	—	1
Notts Co.	(4)	—	—	—	—	—	—	—	—	—	1	2	1	—	—
Coventry	(3)	1	—	—	—	—	1	—	—	1	—	—	—	—	—
Norwich	(3)	—	—	—	2	—	—	—	—	1	—	—	—	—	—
Man. Utd.	(3)	—	—	—	1	—	—	—	1	—	—	1	—	—	—
Middlesbro'	(2)	—	1	—	—	—	—	1	—	—	—	—	—	—	—
Newcastle	(2)	1	1	—	—	—	—	—	—	—	—	—	—	—	—
Chelsea	(2)	1	—	1	—	—	—	—	—	—	—	—	—	—	—
West Ham	(2)	1	—	—	—	—	1	—	—	—	—	—	—	—	—
Bolton	(2)	—	—	—	1	1	—	—	—	—	—	—	—	—	—
Crystal P.	(2)	—	—	—	—	1	—	1	—	—	—	—	—	—	—
Leicester	(1)	—	1	—	—	—	—	—	—	—	—	—	—	—	—
Leeds	(1)	1	—	—	—	—	—	—	—	—	—	—	—	—	—
Q.P.R.	(1)	—	—	—	1	—	—	—	—	—	—	—	—	—	—
Birmingham	(1)	—	—	—	—	—	—	—	—	—	1	—	—	—	—
Southampton	(1)	—	—	—	—	—	—	—	—	—	—	—	1	—	—
Luton	(1)	—	—	—	—	—	—	—	—	—	—	—	—	—	1
		11	9	15	6	7	9	4	4	8	5	14	4	2	2
Goals	(100)	20		21		16		8		13		18		4	
Games	(259)	42		42		42		34		42		42		15	

Gary BAILEY

Talking Football

Gary Bailey, whose hopes of succeeding England's goalkeeper Peter Shilton have taken a setback following some erratic displays this season, offers a fascinating insight into his career with Manchester United, with particular attention given to an Old Trafford defence that has cost the club dearly at times this season...

WHY UNITED'S

Manchester United had the tightest defence in the First Division for two years and it made my job much easier. This season it's all been a problem, and we have leaked in a goal or two we would not have done a couple of seasons ago.

The reason for that is simple: injuries. We have been hit very badly in the back-four — and it is essential for any successful side to have a settled defence. Understanding between them is vital and it only comes with regular partnerships.

This season we have chopped and changed because of injuries … we have had Paul McGrath in and out, Gordon McQueen came back after a long lay-off, Arthur Albiston has been hurt, Kevin Moran and Graeme Hogg have been in and out, and John Gidman and Mike Duxbury have been switching around to shore things up.

I think when Aston Villa won the title, they used 14 players all season … we must have had nearly that many in the defence alone!

DEFENCE HAS CRACKED

I nearly quit

Playing for Manchester United is something really special. There is so much pride at the club, so much pedigree and fine football history, that it is impossible not to feel it.

We all felt it when we played Dundee United and it showed. We battled and we proved we do have a European status — it's important for United to do well in those competitions that bring us into line with the greatest teams in Europe.

The strange thing is that while I'm on top of the world right now, playing in a marvellous side in front of the greatest fans in the world, I nearly left the club six years ago.

I was only third choice when Alex Stepney was injured and forced out of the team. There was a lot of talk about Jim Blyth joining us from Coventry, and he was a really good 'keeper ready to play for Scotland, but I got a chance to show what I could do and almost overnight the entire situation changed.

United battled hard to beat Dundee United in the UEFA Cup.

Extra special Kenny

I have a healthy regard for all strikers, fellows like Joe Jordan, Cyrille Regis and Peter Withe, they are all so big and brave and so good in the air.

But Kenny Dalglish is particularly clever. He and Clive Allen are so quick on the ball that you have to be extremely careful and very watchful when they are within range. Kenny, however, is extra special and you daren't give him an inch of space ... otherwise you're in trouble.

I don't make an absolute study of strikers, but I like to put in a bit of homework before a game to work out what their general strengths and weaknesses are. Which way they take penalties and free-kicks, do they like to cross the ball early or make a late run into the box. That sort of thing.

But even then I don't make it a hard and fast rule that I follow what they *usually* do. I like to leave room for the unexpected.

Concentrate to survive

The secret of goalkeeping is concentration. You can have all the acrobatic agility, know your angles inside out, be brave and strong, but unless you concentrate for the full 90 minutes of any game you can drop an awful clanger.

Goalkeepers are judged on their consistency and it's hard to maintain a level that keeps you on top form all the time — but you have to work at it. And remember my own motto ... React — Don't Anticipate.

Dangerous

Anticipating what a forward is going to do can be very dangerous indeed. He can mis-hit a shot, smash one with what you thought was his weak foot or get a header in when you thought he was useless in the air, and you are in dead trouble.

I much prefer to *react* to what he has done, relying on my reflexes and agility, rather than *guess* what he is going to do and get caught out.

Charlie Nicholas

There's a teenage revolution going on at Highbury and it's threatening us all.

Don Howe's decision to give youth a chance in the Arsenal first team has paid off in a big way because these kids mean business.

Now none of us are safe from the axe, as Graham Rix, Tommy Caton and Steve Williams have all discovered in recent weeks.

To Graham's credit, he reacted in the best possible way when he was dropped following a 6-1 thrashing at Everton in November. No rows, no tantrums. He just knuckled down to working harder than ever in the reserves and has won his place back.

And that's just what Tommy and Steve are having to do while lads like Martin Keown and David Rocastle continue to shine in their places.

The boss has demonstrated to us all that a big transfer fee is no protection against the axe if you're

Arsenal kids a

Niall Quinn
'An ideal partner'

MARTIN KEOWN

DIVISION ONE WINNERS: **Liverpool** ★ FA CUP WINNERS: **Liverpool**

not doing the business.

But that's not the only lesson I've learned from these youngsters. Playing alongside 19-year-old Niall Quinn in the Arsenal attack has made me much more aware of my duties.

Ability

I feel more responsible than ever to get hold of the ball and really do my stuff. And Niall has made it easier for me with his heading ability and tremendous enthusiasm.

The way the team is playing at the moment, Niall's style makes him an ideal partner for me.

We'd tried Chris Whyte up front to lay off the high balls, but when Tony Woodcock and Paul Mariner were both sidelined the boss had no option but to give Niall his chance.

He'd scored 18 goals in 18 reserve games but I think the boss was a little worried about pitching him in too soon. He'd arranged for him to go to Port Vale on loan to gain experience in the lower divisions, but had to call that off when Mariner was injured.

But Don needn't have worried. Niall came in for his League debut against Liverpool — helped by the fact that it was at home — and did all that was asked of him and more.

He was about to sign for Shamrock Rovers when Arsenal stepped in, but Niall could just as easily have made the grade in Gaelic football, hurling or even Australian rules football. Yes, he was offered terms in all three sports!

And just as Niall has helped me to rediscover my form, so Martin Keown is bringing out the best in David O'Leary.

Martin has been a revelation since coming in to replace Tommy Caton. He'd spent six months on loan to Brighton, who tried without success to make the move permanent, but had always been regarded as a right-back before his Arsenal debut in that same 2-0 win against Liverpool.

He's not the biggest lad in the world but is exceptionally sharp on the ground and has developed a great understanding with O'Leary.

Another youngster who's really impressed me is Gus Caesar, a teenaged full-back who stepped in when Viv Anderson was suspended.

Gus missed most of last season with a broken ankle and there were fears for his future.

I took a special interest in his progress because I remember the agony of suffering a broken leg as a teenager and knew just how much hard work was needed to recover.

Those games against Manchester United and QPR were his reward for all that effort.

David Rocastle is one of the most skilful players at the club.

Potential

He's the kind of player crowds get excited about and has bags of potential. David was the first of the youngsters to make the breakthrough this season and has kept battling even though he hasn't been able to hold onto a permanent place.

That's exactly what winger Martin Hayes must do. He came in after the thrashing at Everton in place of Graham Rix but unfortunately we were going through a sticky patch at the time.

Goalless draws with Birmingham and West Brom and a 3-0 defeat at Southampton all co-incided with Martin's run in the team. But he mustn't get disheartened. Martin, you have the ability to succeed at Arsenal. No doubt about it.

That goes for all the lads I've mentioned. They're so keen and so keyed up.

The pressure isn't on them — it's on the 'big name' players who've been left out. That's the great thing about being a young unknown. The crowd give you time to settle in and tolerate any early mistakes.

But these lads have hardly put a foot wrong. They've all been excellent and have proved that they are capable of doing a job in the team.

taught us lesson

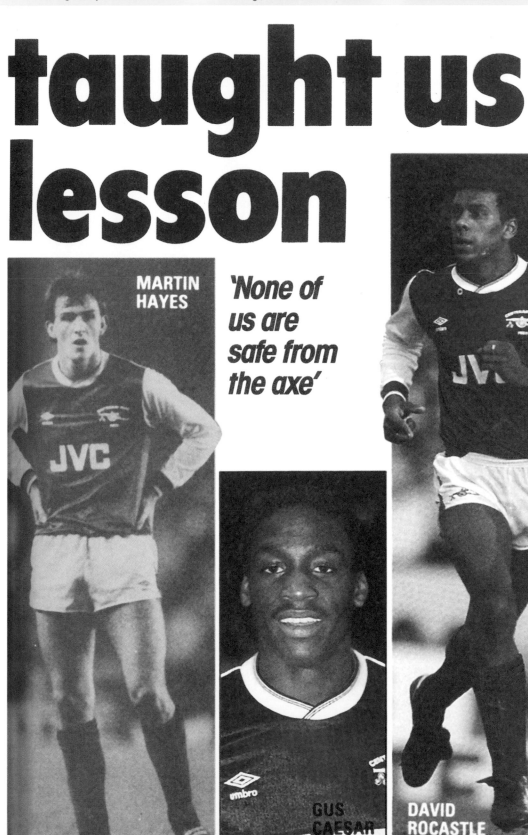

MARTIN HAYES

'None of us are safe from the axe'

GUS CAESAR

DAVID ROCASTLE

I won't go

CLIVE ALLEN, Britain's deadliest striker who slammed 33 First Division goals last season to win the SHOOT/adidas Golden Shoe Award, doesn't *want* to score as many this season.

The Spurs and England striker explains: "Championships are won by teams who share the goals around. All successful sides have strikers who hunt in pairs and players in other positions capable of producing match winners.

"Spurs are now capable of scoring from all angles and if I can return 25 First Division goals this season and Nico Claesen gets 24 I'll be delighted.

"The way the goals went in for me last season was exceptional. There's no way I expected to score 49 overall. The worst thing that happened to me was the summer break. It broke the momentum."

What about opposing defenders? Has Clive been singled out for 'special treatment'?

"By that I suppose you mean am I being kicked more this season. The answer is no," declares Clive.

"There's no way I receive more attention with Nico now playing alongside me. He's a world class striker in his own right and needs watching. He's taken a great deal of weight off me."

Some people reckon Clive is more effective playing his lone raider role. Is Claesen getting in the way?

"We caught clubs out with our tactics last season and it paid off. There's no way we could have played the same way this time.

"David Pleat had to change our style. Nico was staking a claim and couldn't be left out, especially with Glenn Hoddle gone.

"We played together a couple of times last season and the results were good.

"This time we're showing a good goals return between us. We'll get better. You've got to give the partnership time to develop.

"And before you ask, of course we miss Glenn. Who wouldn't? No one can replace him.

"But in a way Glenn's going has helped us become a better side.

It's given other players like Chris Waddle and Nico Claesen the opportunity to establish themselves in their own right.

"Chris has really come out of his shell. He's been playing brilliantly."

Although they've not been playing as well as last season, Tottenham are among the leaders in the First Division. Does Clive seriously consider them Championship material?

"If I didn't I'd quit tomorrow.

"I agree we've not yet shown the form of last season. But don't overlook the different style and system the manager has introduced.

"We must be given the chance to get used to it. With five men in

midfield, Spurs are now extremely difficult to break down. We won't be giving any more silly goals away.

"I read that Manchester United boss Alex Ferguson doesn't believe a London club stands a chance of breaking the Northern dominance.

"What Fergie should remember is that Liverpool, Everton and Manchester United only have two big derbies every season. Spurs will play six other London clubs this season. That's 12 Cup-ties.

EXCLUSIVE

Shoot!/adidas
Golden Shoe winner

The spoils of victory for the striker whose 33 goals last season made him the deadliest First Division marksman for 15 years.

KOP THAT

'The goal I rated best last season was the winner at Liverpool on 11th October. It wasn't a spectacular goal, but it capped a fine team effort.

The move built up from the back when the ball was passed wide to Chris Waddle. He made a great run down the flank and crossed it to the edge of the area. I just managed to get a touch before Bruce Grobbelaar to slip the ball underneath him.'

it alone

By Clive Allen

Allen grabbed 49 goals in all competitions last season, a Spurs record. His exploits earned him the admiration of fans throughout the country, and as well as handing over the Golden Shoe, SHOOT were more than happy to present Clive with the magnificent silver trophy awarded to the player voted the Most Exciting Footballer in England by our thousands of readers.

"I'm sure Spurs have the necessary character and strength to offer the capital's strongest challenge for ten years."

Clive has already established that he puts club before personal targets. But just how much does he want to win this season's Golden Shoe?

"Very much. It's one of the premier awards in the game and is always talked about by strikers.

When I won the Second Division award with QPR in 1979-80 and Phil Boyer collected the Golden Shoe, I made a promise to myself to strike gold.

"But I'll have my work cut out this season. Already Brian

McClair and John Aldridge are staking a claim.

"Kerry Dixon will also be in the reckoning, along with West Ham's Tony Cottee. And don't rule out Nico Claesen. He'd love to get his hands on the trophy."

Another successful spell of goalscoring can't do Clive's England chances any harm.

"It's a burning ambition to add to my four caps, establish myself as England's first choice striker and to play for my country at Wembley.

"To achieve all that means I've got to keep working hard and improve my game."

Will that mean going abroad. Bayern Munich are already reported to offer £1.5 million for him.

"I'd obviously love to play for a top European club," reveals Clive.

"When the time is right and any offer present themselves I'll have to seriously consider them, as would any player.

"Not only would I get financial security for my wife Lisa and son Oliver, but it would enable me to develop my game by playing against some of the world's best.

"Confidence in your own ability is half the battle. And I'd kick myself later if I rejected a golden opportunity."

I'M B

'THE LAST FIVE MONTHS HAVE BEEN THE WORST OF MY LIFE. I THOUGHT I COULD HANDLE A LONG LAY-OFF BUT I WAS WRONG. THE FRUSTRATION DROVE ME UP THE WALL'

AFTER the worst five months of my life, I'm finally ready to make my Rangers return.

And if everything goes according to plan against Hibs this Saturday, I'll be more than happy to offer my services to England manager Bobby Robson for the match against Hungary later this month.

I know that may seem a bit premature, but time is running out for me to prove my fitness in time for the European Championships. Rangers have only four games left this season and England have four lined up before the 20-man squad for the Championships is finalised.

So although I wouldn't dream of picking Mr. Robson's team for him, I feel that I have to play in all those games if I'm going to achieve full match sharpness following my broken leg.

Dave Watson has done a first class job for England in my absence and I thought the criticism levelled at the defence after last month's 2-2 draw with Holland was terribly unfair.

After all, it was the first time that Dave and Tony Adams had played together and I thought they stuck to their task extremely well against a top class Dutch attack.

I don't know if England will take three or four central defenders to the Finals in Germany, but I'm determined to claim one of those places.

So although I don't feel I've reached a make or break situation just yet, I'll still be disappointed if I'm not in the Hungary squad when it's announced next week. At least

TERRY BUTCHER
Column

Alan Hansen's testimonial gives me another game for my diary.

The frustration of such a lengthy lay-off has been driving me up the wall. I thought I could handle it, but I was wrong.

Just how much I've missed the game was driven home to me when I was down at the Lilleshall Rehabilitation Centre and the England squad turned up for fitness tests. I really wanted to join in.

I'd never suffered a broken leg before, so I didn't realise it would take so long to heal.

So although it was agony to miss those clashes against Steaua and the vital League meeting with Celtic, I was determined not to return to action until I was certain my leg was OK.

ACK!

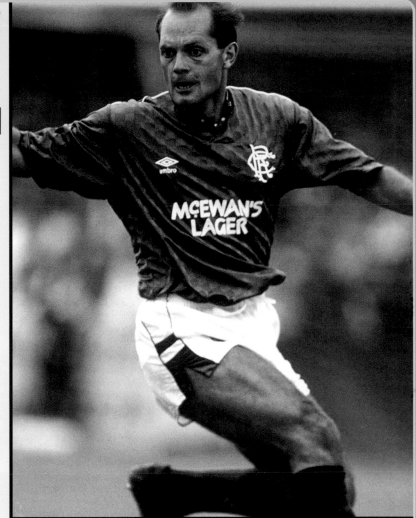

In that respect, Rangers have been marvellous. There has been absolutely no pressure on me to rush back for those three make or break games, even though the defeats have effectively ended our season.

Now I know I'm ready for the tough test ahead. My next big hurdle is my first 50-50 challenge against Hibs at Ibrox, but I won't shirk my responsibility.

Rangers have dropped too many stupid points in defence of our League crown, and although I try to be the eternal optimist I know it will take a monumental cock-up by Celtic for us to be Champions again. They're not that unprofessional to let it slip now.

I haven't exactly been helped by the court case which has been hanging over my head for the last six months.

Doubtless you'll have read that the case was finally heard this week and I hope that's the end of it.

But 1987-88 hasn't been a total disaster for Rangers. Don't forget the Skol Cup we won back in October, and our experiences in Europe will stand us in good stead for next term's UEFA Cup assault.

I'm also looking forward to finally playing in the same team as Ray Wilkins. We've played together through two World Cup Finals, but we're still to appear in the same Rangers side.

Along with Graham Roberts, I'd say that Ray has been our best player this year.

He really felt the pace of the Scottish game after two years in Europe, but he's settled in ever so well and won the fans over in a big way.

He's great with the kids and his wicked sense of humour has me in stitches.

Ray has even been winning headers for the first time in his life, but we've told him he'd better leave the aerial stuff to me because he can't afford to lose any more hair.

We've given him some terrible stick over his bald patch, so now he's taking to wearing a wig in training.

So as you can see, it's not been all doom and gloom at Ibrox in recent months.

You have to give credit to Celtic, Hearts and Aberdeen for the way they have responded to the challenge Rangers threw down last season. But we have got the character to bounce right back next season.

And then we'll really have something to laugh about.

Terry Butcher

SOUR-NESS

It may not be the Glorious Twelfth yet, but up here in Scotland it's definitely Open Season on Graeme Souness.

It's become a way of life to have a go at the gaffer, but in the last few weeks the knives have really come out.

The criticism really got out of hand after our European Cup defeat by Steaua Bucharest. I know it was a bad tackle, but it wasn't as bad as the one committed by Real Madrid's Camacho on the same night against Bayern Munich.

And the incredible quotes falsely attributed to Jan Bartram and given mass exposure in the British Press show just how ready people are to believe anything bad about him.

But the gaffer has done so much for Scottish soccer and he still has a lot to offer the Rangers squad.

I hope he doesn't hang up his boots at the end of the season, because I still want him in front me out on the pitch. He's still very fit and he's a great pro. He's also a big help to the younger members of the team.

Graeme has never been a man to shirk a challenge and I'm sure he won't let this criticism beat him.

I've seen how he handled all the success and adulation last season and now I've seen how he copes with the bad times. And the way he has come through it all has only increased my respect for him.

Graeme Souness is still my Number One. I'm happy to have him as a team-mate and as a manager.

FOCUS ON
DIEGO MARADONA
ARGENTINA

FULL NAME: Diego Armando Maradona
BIRTHPLACE: Lanus (Buenos Aires), Argentina
BIRTHDATE: 30th October, 1960
HEIGHT: 5ft 7ins
WEIGHT: 10st 10lbs
CLUBS: "Las Cebollitas", Argentinos Juniors
MARRIED: No, but I have a steady girlfriend, Claudia
CAR: Ford Coupe — an American model
FAVOURITE PLAYERS: Mario Kempes and Pele
FAVOURITE OTHER TEAM: River Plate
MOST DIFFICULT OPPONENT: Tavita Garcia when he was a River Plate player. Now he's my team-mate at Argentinos
MOST MEMORABLE MATCH: The Semi-Final in the World Youth Championship in Japan, when we beat Uruguay 2-0
BIGGEST THRILL: Winning the World Youth Championship last year, and being voted Sportsman of the Year in Argentina
BIGGEST DISAPPOINTMENT: Missing out on the 1978 World Cup, when Menotti eliminated three players from the squad at the last moment
BIGGEST INFLUENCE ON CAREER: My father in particular, but all my family really
BIGGEST DRAG IN SOCCER: Losing
INTERNATIONAL HONOURS: 20 caps with the Argentina Youth Team, and about 15, I think, with the 'A' team

BEST COUNTRY VISITED: Well, Argentina really, but I like the Brazilian city Rio de Janeiro
FAVOURITE FOOD: Oven-roasted meat
MISCELLANEOUS LIKES: Playing table-tennis and watching TV
MISCELLANEOUS DISLIKES: Injustice
FAVOURITE TV SHOWS: Sports programmes and films
FAVOURITE SINGER: The Spaniard, Julio Iglesias; and melodical music in general
FAVOURITE ACTOR: Ryan O'Neal
BEST FRIEND: Jorge Cyterszpiler, my agent

PERSONAL AMBITION: To be the number one footballer in the world
PROFESSIONAL AMBITION: The same
IF YOU WEREN'T A FOOTBALLER, WHAT DO YOU THINK YOU'D BE? I've no idea. I've always been in football, and it's the most important thing in the world for me
WHICH PERSON IN THE WORLD WOULD YOU MOST LIKE TO MEET? Actress Farah Fawcett

FOCUS ON

PETER BARNES

WEST BROMWICH ALBION

FULL NAME: Peter Simon Barnes
BIRTHPLACE: Manchester
BIRTHDATE: 10th June, 1957
HEIGHT: 5ft. 9ins.
WEIGHT: 11st.
PREVIOUS CLUB: Manchester City
MARRIED: No
CAR: Ford Capri
FAVOURITE PLAYER: George Best
FAVOURITE OTHER TEAM: My former club Manchester City
MOST DIFFICULT OPPONENT: Paul Reaney, formerly Leeds
MOST MEMORABLE MATCH: League Cup Final in 1976
BIGGEST THRILL: Playing for England
BIGGEST DISAPPOINTMENT: None really
BEST COUNTRY VISITED: Switzerland
FAVOURITE FOOD: Indian Curry
MISCELLANEOUS LIKES: Tennis, squash and fishing
MISCELLANEOUS DISLIKES: Smoking and liars
FAVOURITE TV SHOWS: Match of the Day and Fawlty Towers
FAVOURITE SINGERS: ELO and The Eagles
FAVOURITE ACTOR: Paul Newman
BEST FRIEND: Too numerous to mention
BIGGEST INFLUENCE ON CAREER: My father Ken Barnes
BIGGEST DRAG IN SOCCER: Losing
INTERNATIONAL HONOURS: 15 England caps
PERSONAL AMBITION: To be happy in life
PROFESSIONAL AMBITION: A regular England place
IF YOU WEREN'T A FOOTBALLER, WHAT DO YOU THINK YOU'D BE? A PE Teacher
WHICH PERSON IN THE WORLD WOULD YOU MOST LIKE TO MEET? Pele

Peter S Barnes

ON STEVE BRUCE

MAN UTD

How much trouble do you think United are in right now?

We've had some bad results but I don't think we are losing touch with the title race. The First Division is so close this season from top to bottom. It will be won by the team which puts together a ten or 15-match run of results – and naturally I hope that will be us. As for the problems off the pitch, we are just told to keep our minds on the football. They say that whatever happens in the boardroom has nothing to do with us – and they're right when you think about it.

Are you disappointed to have been ignored by Bobby Robson over the last two years?

In a way it is disappointing because when I captained England B in Malta, under Graham Taylor, it was my first England involvement since winning Youth caps. I thought I played quite well – we won 2-0 – but that was that. I thoroughly enjoyed the experience and I hope it won't be my last. All you can do is keep plugging away and I'm pretty happy with my form right now. But realistically I can't see much chance of making the England plane to Italy. I think Bobby Robson is looking

at players younger than myself who are coming through. I won't write myself off – but I'll probably have to go to Italy on holiday in order to see the World Cup.

With all the traumas at United, do you ever regret leaving Norwich?

No. I would have crawled to Manchester to join United and I don't regret signing, however well Norwich have done in my absence. I would be lying if I said I wasn't surprised by the way The Canaries reached the Semi-Finals of the FA Cup and nearly won the Championship last season. But they are doing it again in the League, which proves what a good footballing side Norwich have. However, games against them are often the lowest point of a top-flight club's season, while fixtures against United are like Cup

Finals. So we have to be on top of our form at all times. I love playing in front of 40,000 and 50,000 crowds and I wouldn't change a thing. I have learned how to take the pressure but I can see why some lads come to Old Trafford and never fulfil their true potential.

What is your biggest ambition now?

To win something with United. Of course, if another England opportunity came up then that would be marvellous too.

How would you describe your partnership with Gary Pallister?

I think it is getting better. Unfortunately I was injured when he first arrived and Gary will admit that he found life difficult to start with. It is hard enough to be labelled a great player without having a £2.3 million price tag on your head. But now he is coming on and he will improve even more. It always takes time to get a working relationship together and I don't see any major problems for the future. On a personal note I certainly don't begrudge him the England recognition he has had – good luck to him.

1990 The year at a glance... DIVISION ONE WINNERS: Liverpool ★ FA CUP WINNERS: Manchester United

Middlesbrough goal ace Bernie Slaven will end the international arguments when he makes his debut for the Republic of Ireland against Wales at Lansdowne Road next Wednesday.

Scotland boss Andy Roxburgh was furious when Jack Charlton named Paisley-born Slaven in his squad for the Wales game an incredible six weeks ago.

Roxburgh claimed he was planning to give the 25-goal hot-shot a Scotland call-up until the Irish made the unprecedented move of announcing their squad so far in advance.

But Slaven insists: "With all

SHAMROCK SLAVEN

Bernie joins the Eire Force

due respect to Scotland, they had plenty of opportunity to give me a chance. After all, I'd played for Morton, Airdrie, Queen of the South and Albion Rovers before joining Boro five years ago.

"It was only when my Irish connections became public knowledge that Mr Roxburgh showed any interest in me."

Slaven will become the 40th player to be capped in Charlton's four-year reign when the Welsh visit Dublin.

And Bernie reveals: "I chose the Republic because Jack Charlton said he was prepared to give me a chance against Wales while Andy Roxburgh could not promise me a full senior game.

"I do have an Irish grandfather, so why not declare for the land of my ancestors? I know that the other British-born lads who have declared for the Republic have been made very welcome by the Irish fans.

"They were very patient when John Aldridge went through a barren spell and hopefully they will give me a fair trial."

Ironically, it could be Aldridge who feels the pressure most from Slaven's arrival as the race for World Cup places hots up.

For while Aldo has been a scoring sensation in Spain with Real Sociedad, at international level his record is a paltry three goals in 28 games so far.

Says Charlton: "Bernie is the type of player who could benefit from Tony Cascarino's knock downs.

"We've been a bit short of strikers for a while, but this lad's scoring record for Middlesbrough this season has been tremendous and so we must see if he can do it at international level."

At the age of 29, Slaven will be one of the oldest international debutants of all time. But a trip to Italy is within his grasp and a good performance against the Welsh next week should be enough to claim that prize.

★ The 'B' international between Ireland and England at Cork's Turner's Cross ground has been made an all-ticket match with a capacity of 10,000. The only League of Ireland player likely to feature in the match is St.Patrick's Athletic right-back Curtis Fleming.

★ The Republic have lost only once in Dublin under Jack Charlton's management. That was in his first game in charge against Wales, back in March 1986. Ireland's full home record under Big Jack reads: P18 W12 D5 L1 F31 A5.

★ Ray Houghton, who picked up his second yellow card in the World Cup win over Malta, is likely to sit out this game and be ready to resume his international career against the USSR next month.

★ Wales and Eire have met four times previously, with Wales winning all four games.

DIVISION ONE WINNERS: Arsenal ★ FA CUP WINNERS: Tottenham

DON'T GO DES

Stay with me at Forest

D es Walker was treated like a King when he was in Italy last summer – and it's no secret that he'd pick up a King's Ransom if he ever went there to play his club football.

I was in Italy with him twice – once with England and again when we went on a pre-season tour with Forest – and on both occasions he was followed everywhere by Press and supporters alike.

I don't know whether he'll end up in Italy eventually but there's no doubt that all the top clubs out there are now aware of his talent.

I've been lucky enough to play with him in the vast majority of his games for both Forest and England – and, believe me, he's all he's cracked up to be.

He's not only like grease lightning off the mark but when you add his speed of thought as well, somebody has got to be going some to get past him.

What you also find with Des is that he always stands his ground and invites attackers to beat him. He doesn't commit himself by diving into tackles.

The fans at Forest have got this chant

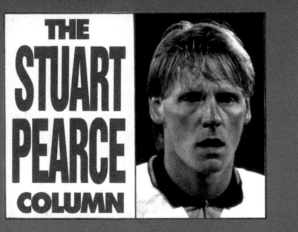

THE STUART PEARCE COLUMN

"You'll never beat Des Walker" and over the years not many people have.

With his appearances for England and his growing reputation, it's not difficult to understand why he's been labelled world class and why the Italians have been chasing him.

It's none of my business what happens on the transfer front but suffice to say that having committed myself to Forest for the next five years, I would be delighted to see Des by my side throughout that time.

Keane is Mustard

R oy Keane has come from nowhere this season to establish himself in the First Division with Forest.

But he was such a surprise packet to me I thought he was playing for the opposition when he made his debut against Liverpool!

I was out injured for his first match at Anfield and when I read the following morning that Keane had made an impressive debut, I can remember thinking to myself: "That's a new Liverpool player I haven't heard about."

We're all delighted for him at the City Ground that he's gone into the side as an unknown 19-year-old and stayed there.

What's more, he's more than held his own and what with the injuries we've had this season, we would have been a bit stretched to say the least had he not come in and done so well.

He's also building a reputation for himself as a goalscorer and I would have been thrilled to bits with the two strikes that brought him goals in our 6-2 win at Norwich. His second was an absolute scorcher from well outside the box.

The great thing about Roy is that he appears to be level headed. I say "appears" because nobody can really understand his particular brand of Irish.

Seriously though, he's sensible enough to realise he's still going to face fresh challenges in the future but from what we've seen of him so far, he'll be a name that will be around for a long time – playing for Nottingham Forest not Liverpool.

SHOOT readers grill Anfield boss
SOUNESS

Graeme Souness *never ducked a challenge as a player and the same steely qualities which have carried him through his first few years as a manager came in handy when he was given the third degree by SHOOT readers. We asked if you had any questions to put to the Liverpool boss; you replied in your hundreds...and pulled no punches either. We're grateful to Graeme for ploughing through your stack of mail. Here are his replies...it's another SHOOT exclusive!*

YOU WERE AN INSPIRATION AS LIVERPOOL SKIPPER, BUT DO YOU FIND IT MORE DIFFICULT TO EXERT THE SAME INFLUENCE AS A MANAGER FROM THE DUG-OUT?
(John Collins, Cavan, Rep.of Ireland)
It's far easier to be influential when you are out on the pitch and I would much rather still be playing because actions speak louder than words. As a manager you do your bit before a game and at half-time, but once the players are out on the pitch you can't have that much influence – especially at Anfield! The atmosphere is such that you can't make yourself heard and your messages don't get across.

WHAT IS IT LIKE TO MANAGE A TOP CLUB LIKE LIVERPOOL?
(James Taylor, Huddersfield, W.Yorks)
It involves a lot more work than people appreciate - not just what you do between 3pm and 4.40 on a Saturday. These days the various aspects of the job are more time-consuming than ever before. For instance, I'm trying to answer all these letters for you before I have to rush off to a game at Newcastle tonight.

WHAT QUALITIES MAKE A LIVERPOOL FOOTBALLER BETTER THAN ANY OTHER?
(Martin Clark, Gypsy Hill, S.London)
Liverpool play the game the way it should be played. Our beliefs lie in passing and movement, not in the goalkeeper kicking it as far as he can...and a big centre-forward just charging about. It's not something that's happened overnight, it's been an on-going situation here since the 60s and the players we bring to Anfield reflect the club's policies.

WHO DO YOU THINK HAS BEEN THE FINEST PLAYER EVER TO PLAY FOR LIVERPOOL?
(Kirsty Grogan, Stamford, Lincs)
A lot of good judges around here have always rated a famous Scottish forward from the 40s and 50s called Billy Liddell as very special. But there was more to him than being a great player. He was a miner's son who taught himself to be an accountant, when he retired he became a magistrate and he also worked hard on behalf of youth organisations. Of the players I've seen, Kenny Dalglish has to be the finest. He was as willing to be a team member as he was an individual - you really can't emphasise that point enough.

IF YOU HAD TO SELL JOHN BARNES, HOW MUCH WOULD YOU SELL HIM FOR?
(Tim Pyerson, Cowley, Oxford)
What 'I'd like to get' and what 'I will get' are two entirely different things. It's like when you sell your house, you ask for as much as you could possibly get. But I'm not thinking about a fee because I don't want to sell John Barnes; I want him to stay and I shall be doing everything in my power to keep him at Liverpool.

'I will do everything in my power to keep John Barnes'

'Kenny Dalglish is the greatest player I've seen'

'I happen to think David James is a quality player'

WHY HAVE YOU SOLD PLAYERS OF THE CALIBRE OF PETER BEARDSLEY AND STEVE McMAHON AND WHAT DOES THE IMMEDIATE FUTURE HOLD FOR BRUCE GROBBELAAR?
(Dean Spencer, Loughborough)...
DO YOU THINK YOU HAVE MADE THE RIGHT SIGNINGS?
(G.J.Sheil, Banbury, Essex).
I'm certainly happy with the players I have signed (Dean Saunders, Mark Wright, Rob Jones and Michael Thomas) although I don't think any manager is ever completely happy with his squad. He is always looking to improve it. If that means chopping and changing players then I'll do so; that's what I get paid for. It's my job to have a squad of players who want to die for the club. I'm only interested in people who have Liverpool FC totally at heart. As regards the goalkeeping situation, we are always interested in quality players when they become available and I happen to think David James is a quality player.

FOUR

'We'll get it right this time' …'this will be our ye[ar]
you've heard it all before about Manchester Uni[ted]
title. But this time the boys from Old Trafford [mean it]
and SHOOT throws the spotlight on the men Al[ex Ferguson]
will end the club's 25-year Championship drough[t]

SHARPE:
The Comeback Kid

'He's better than ever'

Graeme Souness once likened the return from injury of Rangers ace Ian Durrant to 'signing a £3m player'. Alex Ferguson knows how he felt.

In fact the United boss feels he's got a player money can't buy in comeback kid Lee Sharpe.

Illness and injury sent the England winger into the depths of despair and put his promising career on the line. But now he's back and buzzing…and so are United.

"Lee is a better player now than when he was capped by England," enthuses Fergie. "He doesn't flatter, he delivers. He produces crosses when you want them and is more than a reasonable finisher.

"I think being out of the side did him good because he watched carefully and, when he returned, surprised us with his knowledge of the game."

Sharpe, having emerged from the worst year of his life with that beaming smile intact, agrees with his boss.

"It was a shocking time and there were many occasions when I thought my form was never going to return," Lee recalls. "Yet looking back now I know I learned a lot.

"I feel a different player and have taken on more responsibility. I used to just sit on the full-back but I get back into midfield more now."

Sharpe's personal determination is being matched by his team-mates as they step up their title bid and he says: "There's a strong resolve inside the squad and you can sense a feeling of 'we've got to win it this time'."

McCLA[IR]

'He is abs[olutely brilliant]'

Brian McClair has been put in [a new role]
but Manchester United's 'Mr Ver[satility']

That's the view of Alex Fergus[on whose]
player often made the scapegoat[.]

Fergie insists McClair, playing i[n]
Cantona, is 'perfect' for United a[t]

"I hold up my hands to Brian be[cause]
Fergie. "He is a United man throu[gh and through]
ask of him without a moan.

"He doesn't catch the eye as m[uch but]
everyone appreciates his contribu[tion]
he is absolutely brilliant."

Unlike some players under thre[at]
faced with the prospect of losing [his place to the]
Frenchman.

He just got on with his job, vow[ing]
place - wherever it might be.

Says McClair: "There is now a lo[t of]
competition for places. But it doe[sn't]
or in midfield.

"I'd love to keep my place as a s[triker]
says. We all welcomed the arrival [of Cantona]

ON THE SPOT

'I'm only interested in people who have Liverpool FC totally at heart'

DOES IAN RUSH FIGURE IN YOUR FUTURE PLANS? (J.Westcott, Sussex)
When Ian Rush is fit I am sure that, if his desire returns along with his fitness, he will get in any team that I was going to pick. I think a Saunders-Rush partnership can succeed up front. They are both proven goalscorers at every level.

DO YOU STILL BELIEVE LIVERPOOL CAN WIN THE CHAMPIONSHIP? (Mark Taylor, Bootle, Merseyside)
We're around the halfway mark and we've had a disastrous first half in terms of injuries. I would hate to think the rest of the season would turn out the same way, but we can't guarantee that it won't. As far as the League is concerned, we will fight for every

'The best teams don't always win the trophies'

point until the last ball of the season is kicked…come what may. But football is such that the best teams don't always win the trophies.

WILL LIVERPOOL EVER BE AS SUCCESSFUL IN EUROPE WITH THE NEW REGULATIONS ON 'FOREIGN' PLAYERS? (S.Parsons, Wellington, Somerset)
It is a problem for all English clubs – especially Liverpool because we've always had a fair sprinkling of Irish, Welsh and Scottish players. It simply makes the job that much harder, but by no means impossible.

WHO IS THE BEST PLAYER AT ANFIELD AT THE MOMENT? (Dean Gwyn, Gwent)
I believe I have a squad containing so many excellent footballers that I couldn't begin to pick just one. You cannot say one player is better than another because they all play in different positions. What I would say is that we have some of the best players in the country at this club.

'I would much rather be playing than managing'

FERGIE'S

CANTONA:
The great entertainer

INCE

'He can be as big as Best'

Alex Ferguson reckons Eric Cantona can become the biggest Old Trafford star since George Best.

Fergie is convinced that United and Cantona are perfect for each other and that the fiery Frenchman has the Midas touch to finally put an end to the club's Championship agony.

"There have been many players with what people call 'temperament' who have played for United and distinguished themselves," says Fergie. "Eric Cantona will be no exception.

"He is a great entertainer, just like George Best was, with a feel for the game. I'm confident about the success of his transfer because United are tailor-made for a player of his nature.

"They don't call Old Trafford the theatre of dreams for nothing. We have a unique stage here just right for his talents and I believe he can help us win the title.

"He is smart enough to realise that United can satisfy him emotionally and I have promised him that he will never forget playing for this club."

Eric the Red's new strike partner Mark Hughes underlines his manager's view that Cantona can be the club's lucky mascot.

"He arrived at Leeds and had a real influence on their Championship success," says the Welshman. "He can do the same for us.

"For a big man Eric's touch is amazing and he has impressed everyone here already. He is going to make a big difference to our season."

'He can

Paul Ince is enjoying his be be called 'The New Robbo'...

A suspect temperament an Jagger threatened to keep th

But now, with a key role to showing the maturity and m

The former East End rebel, grown up and says: "Being p influence on me. But it was t major turning point. I had to

"There were so many occas consumed by the will to win that such behaviour is not go

"I'm really trying to keep m certainly improved in terms o

That has not been overlook fulfilling the potential we sav

"He's been a bit of a late de and will get even better. Bein

"Now he must look to estab he first came to Manchester Robson goes, is to become th

MARK HATELEY

SHOOT **adidas** *Golden Shoe winner Scottish Premier 1993-94*

How the goals went in

Opponents	League games	Goals
Aberdeen	4	2
Celtic	4	1
Dundee	4	1
Dundee Utd	4	1
Hearts	4	6
Hibernian	4	1
Kimarnock	4	2
Motherwell	3	1
Patrick	4	1
Raith	4	2
St Johnstone	3	4
TOTAL	**42**	**22**

Hateley also scored four Scottish Cup goals (v Dumbarton, Hearts and Kilmarnock 2), two Scottish League Cup goals (v Aberdeen and Celtic) and two European Cup goals (v Levski Sofia) to take his season's tally to 30.

Mark Hateley capped a memorable season when he was named as the Scottish Football Writers' Player of the Year - the first Englishman ever to win the award.

Add that to the Players' Player of the Year award and the SHOOT/adidas Golden Shoe and you can see why Hateley is rated as the best hit-man north of the border.

With Ally McCoist missing for long periods of the season, Hateley took over the Ibrox goalscoring mantle - and how.

He blasted 22 League goals as Rangers swept to their sixth successive title triumph and says: "I had to change my role because we were without Ally and I had to be more of an out-and-out striker. I had to be more greedy and selfish."

It clearly worked and, despite the disappointment of losing the Scottish Cup Final to Dundee United and missing out on an history making second successive treble, Hateley can't wait to get started again.

"I have signed a new three-year contract at Rangers and being named Player of the Year has given me a real lift. It was a great honour.

"I hope to stay at the very top until the end of my career and I'm told that Terry Venables has spoken to Walter Smith so I may even get another England chance."

On the Mark

Name: Mark Hateley
Birthdate: November 7, 1961
Birthplace: Liverpool
Height: 6ft 1in
Weight: 11st 7lbs

Club Record
Coventry: 25 goals in 93 games
Portsmouth: 22 goals in 38 games
AC Milan: 17 goals in 66 games
Monaco: 22 goals in 59 games
Rangers: 72 goals in 139 games

International record
Nine goals in 32 full England appearances

Transfers
May 1983: Coventry to Portsmouth £190,000
June 1984: Portsmouth to AC Milan £915,000
June 1987: AC Milan to Monaco £2 million
June 1990: Monaco to Rangers £500,000

Milestones
Hateley made his mark on the world scene when he scored for England against Brazil in 1984 and was instantly snapped up by AC Milan.

Mark Hateley has added a fourth award to his list of accolades. He's already been hailed as the Scottish Football Writers' Player of the Year and the Players' Player of the Year. And now he's picked up the award for SHOOT's Most Exciting Player of the Year in Scotland. Here's how you voted...

Player	No. of Votes
1 Mark Hateley	741
2 Pat McGinlay	312
3 Eoin Jess	306
4 Duncan Shearer	228
5 Tommy Coyne	150
6 Roddy Grant	123

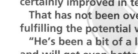

Crown Duals

Who will be Kings of the double-act?

So, the auction is over and Chris Sutton is a Blackburn player. And the Ewood Park club has a strike pair worth £8.3 million, but how will it compare with the top flight's other hot-shots? SHOOT takes a look at the Premiership's dynamic duos...

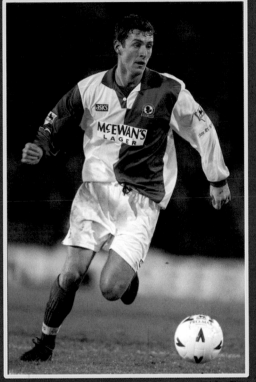

Fifty-six goals is the target which the most expensive strikeforce in British soccer history will have to reach if they are to prove they're the best double act around.

Newcastle's Andy Cole and Peter Beardsley combined to hit 55 strikes in the Premier League last term and that's the target Alan Shearer and his new Blackburn buddy Chris Sutton have set their sights on.

And it will prove a tough task as we reveal that, Cole and Beardsley apart, most strikeforces have a lousy first season in front of goal.

Here's the run down on the leading Premier partnerships Sutton and Shearer will rival for top billing.

Alan Shearer & Chris Sutton

If these two hit it off, the rest of the country is going to be in serious trouble. Shearer is the best striker in England and the only doubt is whether Sutton is too similar to him. Only time will tell but if it works, then Kenny Dalglish will be rubbing his hands with glee. And so will Terry Venables.

Goal Potential (out of 10): 10
League goals last season: Shearer 23; Sutton (Norwich) 25 = Total 48

Mark Hughes & Eric Cantona

The classic silk and steel combination. Nobody gets the better of Hughes when it comes to a physical battle, while Cantona can win a game on his own with one flash of individual genius. They helped United win the double last season and it will take something special to stop them doing it again.

Goal Potential: 10
Total goals first season together: 24.
Second season: 30
Total: 54

Andy Cole & Peter Beardsley

The way they played last season you would have thought they had been a partnership all their lives, instead of just a few months. Cole's explosive pace makes him a constant threat, while Beardsley can see passes the rest of us can only dream about (apart from our own Steve Pearce, that is!). The Geordie Gems have got goals written all over them.

Goal Potential: 10
Total goals first season together: 55.

Ian Wright & Kevin Campbell

There's no doubting Wright's ability, but we are still waiting for Campbell to live up to his potential. Wright has been Arsenal's main man for the past two seasons, and will always score goals. Now it's time for Campbell to assume his share of the responsibility.

Goal Potential: 9
Total goals first season together: 37.
Second season: 21
Third season: 37
Total: 95

Les Ferdinand & Bradley Allen

Ferdinand has burst to the fore in the last couple of seasons and is right up there with the likes of Shearer and Wright. He's had his share of different partners in the past couple of seasons, but these two - with Ferdy's power and Allen's eye for goal - look to be QPR's best bet.

Goal Potential: 8
Total goals first season together: 30
Second season: 24
Total: 54

Ian Rush & Robbie Fowler

They've been billed as Rush Mark I and Rush Mark II and there's no question that they have similar qualities, mainly that they keep scoring goals. Fowler could be Liverpool's main striker for the next ten years, but how long Rush can hang in there with him is another matter.

Goal Potential: 7
Total goals first season together: 26.

Mark Bright & David Hirst

These two have hardly played together because of Hirst's continued injury problems, but you'd certainly fancy them to score goals. If they get the right service the pair could once again make an impact although Hirst will need to be at his best if he is to spearhead a battle with Sutton and Shearer.

Goal Potential: 7
Goals first season together: 22
Second season: 20
Total: 42.

* Partnership figures taken from total goals of individual players for each season in the League

DOUBLE DUTCH

● He was born in Surinam on 1st September 1962. His father was a Surinam soccer international and his mother was Dutch.

● Ruud made his debut for FC Haarlem as a 16-year-old in 1978 and went on to win his first cap - as sub for Frank Rijkaard - in a game against Switzerland in 1981.

● Johann Cruyff signed the young Gullit for Feyenoord, and the player helped the side to the League and Cup double in 1984.

● Close rivals PSV Eindhoven lured Gullit away in 1985, and the dreadlocked superstar grabbed 48 goals in 68 games as PSV won two titles in two seasons.

● In 1987 he was named European Footballer of the Year, tempting Milan to fork out £5.7 million for his services.

● 1988 was a golden year for Ruud, as he helped Holland to land the European Championship.

● A knee injury put him out of action for some time, but he returned to score a sensational goal in the 1989 European Cup Final as Milan beat Steaua 4-0.

● In 1993, Gullit transferred to Sampdoria for £5 million where he formed a lethal partnership with England's David Platt.

● After a year at Samp he rejoined Milan for a short spell before returning again to Sampdoria. The club awarded him a free transfer at the end of last season as a 'thank you' for his services.

● Ruud had many offers from other European clubs, and also a big money deal to go to Japan. But as a big fan of English football and Glenn Hoddle he chose Chelsea.

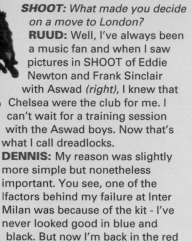

SHOOT: *What made you decide on a move to London?*
RUUD: Well, I've always been a music fan and when I saw pictures in SHOOT of Eddie Newton and Frank Sinclair with Aswad *(right)*, I knew that Chelsea were the club for me. I can't wait for a training session with the Aswad boys. Now that's what I call dreadlocks.
DENNIS: My reason was slightly more simple but nonetheless important. You see, one of the Ifactors behind my failure at Inter Milan was because of the kit - I've never looked good in blue and black. But now I'm back in the red and white of my beloved Ajax, I couldn't be happier.

SHOOT: *Is that why you turned down Aston Villa then?*
DENNIS: Yes, all this talk of my refusing to take a drop in wages is nonsense. The simple truth is that Villa wouldn't change their kit.

SHOOT: *Was it a tough decision to make to come to England?*
RUUD: Well, obviously you have to sit down carefully and weigh up all the pros and cons of moving to another country. You have to be sure that you will be able to adapt to the lifestyle and there are a lot of things to be considered. It needs a lot of thought.
DENNIS: No, I just hated Italy!

SHOOT: *What are you most looking forward to next season?*
RUUD: I'm very keen to go shopping down the King's Road and it will be wonderful to be part of the London club scene.
SHOOT: Yes quite, but what about on the pitch?
RUUD: Oh sorry. Well, it will be a thrill to finally meet the world famous Stamford the Lion.

Over here, Ruud!

DENNIS: I've always admired the work of Alan Smith and I thought he was desperately unlucky to be sacked by Crystal Palace. But now I will have the chance to form a striking partnership with him at

BERGKAMP ON GULLIT

"Ruud is one of the great Dutch players of all time. He is a legend and I have learned much from playing in the same side, and also against him in Italy. He is still a world class player with a lot of experience to add to his skill"

Jurgen Klinsmann may have gone, but the capital will still boast two world superstars next season. IAN CRUISE tracked down Ruud Gullit and Dennis Bergkamp and he was stunned by what they told him. We had no idea they were such top blokes and here, in one of the most amazing interviews ever, they talk of their hopes for the future...

...and it certainly is!

Highbury and I couldn't be more excited. (Eh?! - Ed)

SHOOT: *What do you know of your respective managers?*
RUUD: Everyone knows that Glenn Hoddle was one of the most gifted artists of his generation. It was always a pleasure to see him in action. His performance on Top of the Pops singing Diamond Lights will live long in the memory.
DENNIS: I didn't even realise Bruce Rioch had gone into football management. He is well known in Holland for his role in the Generation Game, but he certainly seems to have changed his appearance - has he had a face-lift? I was very disappointed that, when I arrived, he didn't say 'nice to see you, to see you, nice'.

SHOOT: *Do you know much about your new team-mates?*
RUUD: Not a lot, I must admit. But I was told that if I go out on the town with Dennis Wise I should go by tube, rather than getting a taxi. I don't know what all that is about.
DENNIS: Like Ruud, I don't know too much about individuals, although I have played against Tony Adams and David Seaman for Holland. And I also know Arsenal have a reputation for playing excellent, free-flowing football.

SHOOT: *What will you miss most about Italy?*
RUUD: It was nice that we played on Sundays because that meant I could take the wife shopping on a Saturday. She used to enjoy that, but now it looks as though she will have to go to Kwiksave on her own.
DENNIS: I will miss the food because those guys sure know how to use some spaghetti and a few meatballs. But I'm told there's a cracking little Italian restaurant in Islington so I'll be nipping down there whenever I can.

SHOOT: *Do you think we will see more and more Dutch players coming to England?*
RUUD: We see a lot of English football on TV in Holland and we are all great admirers of the Premiership, especially the skills and techniques of players like... erm...err... oh, you know who I mean.
DENNIS: I understand that Marc Overmars interests a couple of your clubs and he would do very well in England. I'm not sure Des Walker would be too keen to see him, though. And I gather that Ajax captain Danny Blind is wanted by Aston Villa. They would be alright for him because he's never had any dress sense.

SHOOT: *Do you expect to win things here?*
RUUD: I fully expect to be named Football of the Year. I hear that all you have to do is score a few goals and dive around a bit and they give it to you. Then they let you go home.
DENNIS: As long as Brucie lets me have a cuddly toy I will be happy. Anything else will a bonus.

SHOOT: *Well, thanks very much guys it's been very...err...interesting*

Nice to see you Den

KNVB

lotto

GULLIT ON BERGKAMP

"He has proved himself to be one of the best players in the world. He is a very clever and intelligent player who can set goals up as well as being a deadly finisher. He is a big hero in Holland and was very popular in Italy."

England's Euro 96 heroes - PAUL GASCOIGNE in particular - have proved that they are capable of competing with the best in Europe. Now Gazza's sights are set on the World Cup and his rivals had better beware as the Geordie genius declares......

WE CAN TAKE ON THE WORLD

"It goes without saying that we are all gutted to have lost out in another penalty shoot-out with the Germans - especially the few of us who went through the same heartbreak in Italy six years ago.

But no-one can argue with the fact that we went out of Euro 96 with our heads held high, and I'll tell you this...the rest of the world had better watch out because this is only the start.

We proved against Germany, and even more so against Holland - two of the tournament favourites - that we can live and compete with the best ...both in terms of commitment and technique.

The England team had its doubters and more than a few critics, notably amongst some of the tabloid Press, in the build-up to the tournament but they soon changed their tune, didn't they?

Even before a ball was kicked we felt we were capable of going all the way to the Final and, with such fantastic support behind us at Wembley each time, our confidence grew with every game.

It's just a shame that we couldn't have rewarded our magnificent fans with a victory against Germany and another memorable Wembley occasion. Who knows what would have happened next.

But at least we made our exit from the tournament playing football the way it should be played. Terry Venables said we deserved better and who can argue with that statement?

We proved a lot of people wrong and made a lot more sit up and take notice. The performance against Holland was as good as anything I've been involved in. And the atmosphere was incredible.

From a personal point of view, it was great to show people I can still perform on the biggest stage. And that I'm not the 'burned out wreck' some people would have you believe.

I played a full season in Scotland - winning virtually everything for Rangers - and I only failed to finish one of England's games in Euro 96.

Two of those games went to extra-time and penalties and yet I was still going strong. Burned out? Don't make me laugh.

Of course it was tough, both physically and mentally, and there were

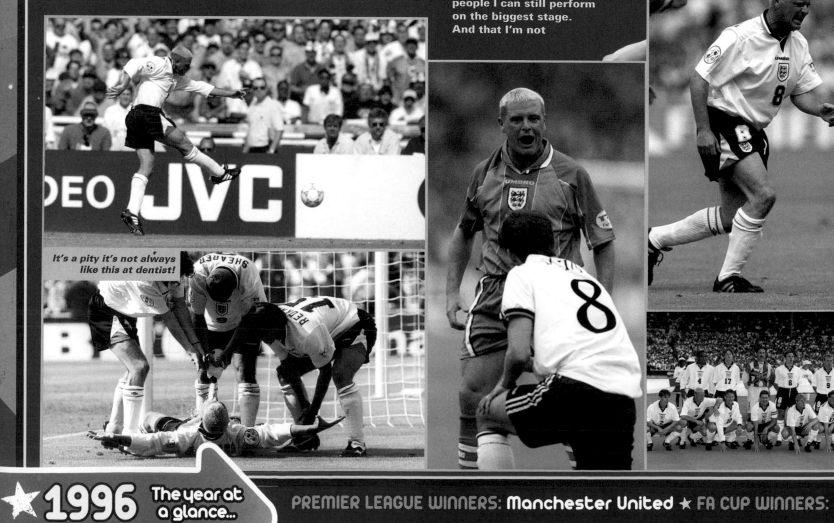

It's a pity it's not always like this at dentist!

I told him I appreciated everything Leeds had done. His reaction was okay on the phone.

But then he had a go at you in the papers and virtually called you a liar, didn't he?

Yeah. I wanted to let rip back but I'm pleased I didn't. I wanted to put the record straight for my family, myself and everyone. There was no point though because Bill probably made his comments in the heat of the moment.

If Liverpool go on to win the League, how will you feel?

I will be pleased for the lads, the club and the supporters. The players deserve it. But secretly I will be very envious. Success is what we all want to be part of but I made a decision and I've no regrets now.

But Spurs haven't got a squad capable of winning the title.

Well I think they have. The squad is definitely capable. There's all sorts of things to get right but the players here are right. The likes of Anderton, Armstrong, Sheringham, and now Vega and Iversen...the talent is there.

What chance of you getting back in the England set-up again, then?

I'm ambitious and want to be part of the England set-up but I've not been fit since Glenn Hoddle took over and I've taken a step back since last season when I played in the FA Cup Final. I learned a hell of a lot over the years I was at Liverpool, especially playing in Europe, and of course, I want to be part of the World Cup squad.

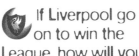

I'll have to play with Clive Wilson? No!!

times when we needed the crowd to keep us going but there's bottle as well as talent in this England team.

Nobody displayed it more than Stuart Pearce, who was an inspiration to us all. But that's what we have come to expect from the man. He typified the spirit in the squad.

As we said, we were all in it together and Glenn Hoddle will take over a group of players who will always give 110 per cent for the cause, for each other....and those superb fans.

It's just a shame Glenn won't be in charge of the European Champions because that's what we deserve to be. We came so close it's agonising to think about it.

Few people came closer to putting us in the Final than me. I was only inches away from scoring the Golden Goal winner which would have sent us, not Germany, into a showdown with the Czechs.

We don't need reminding it was the same scenario in Italia 90. It just wasn't meant to be. Maybe next time.

MY MESSAGE TO THE FANS

The support at Wembley for all five games was incredible; the best I've ever known. You could actually feel the crowd willing us on.

I've played in stadiums all over the world, but there's nothing like Wembley on occasions like that. The atmosphere was something special.

It really gave us a boost to know that everyone was right behind us and it makes me proud to think we gave so much pleasure to so many people.

I'm just sorry we couldn't have kept the smiles - and the songs -

going a little bit longer. The thought of playing in the Final in front of all those wonderful fans sends a tingle down your spine.

Sadly, we didn't make it all the way but, like Italia 90, it was an experience I'll never forget.

In Italy, the celebration song of the fans was 'Let's all have a disco' and that was great. But hearing the Wembley fans singing 'Football's Coming Home' was something else.

Thanks to everyone for their support. Come back and do it all again when we start the World Cup campaign. Your country needs you....

Gazza

WE SALUTE TEL'S LION KINGS

SHOOT

WE'RE PROUD OF YOU ALL

Gazza Exclusive • Shearer Tribute • Euro 96 Extra

Sca...

Why Spurs and why no...

On the Thursday he's at Anfield, on t... sign for Leeds. But on the Sunday, he... joining Tottenham. Four whirlwind days... Scales' life. So tell us about it Scales...

Did you really want to leave Liverpool then, Scalesy?

No, I didn't want to leave. I was quite happy there and only half-way through a five year contract. I thought I played really well over the two-and-half years I was there. But this season I picked up a calf injury and came back to fitness not fully right. I hadn't been in the team but I felt part of the squad and was very happy there, though.

Was it a shock to move then?

Yeah...totally out of the blue. There had been no indication from the club that they were looking to sell me. I think it was down to circumstances that Leeds came in, made the offer and Roy Evans told me Liverpool had accepted it at about four or five o'clock on the Thursday evening.

Did you feel hurt that they were... ready to let you go?

I suppose it did, yes. I can't lie... say anything different. I felt tha... for a club to accept the offer tol... me everything. I did question w... they were prepared to let me g... that particular time, what with... Liverpool still being involved in... competitions and that.

What was the conversation with Roy like?

It was good. You have to remember he's working for the... club and it's not his decision al... But he basically said I had permission to speak to Leeds a... they were not saying I had to g... He told me if I wanted to see... contract out, they were happy... me to stay at Liverpool and figh... for my place.

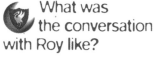

You looking at me, pal?

The o... John... that...

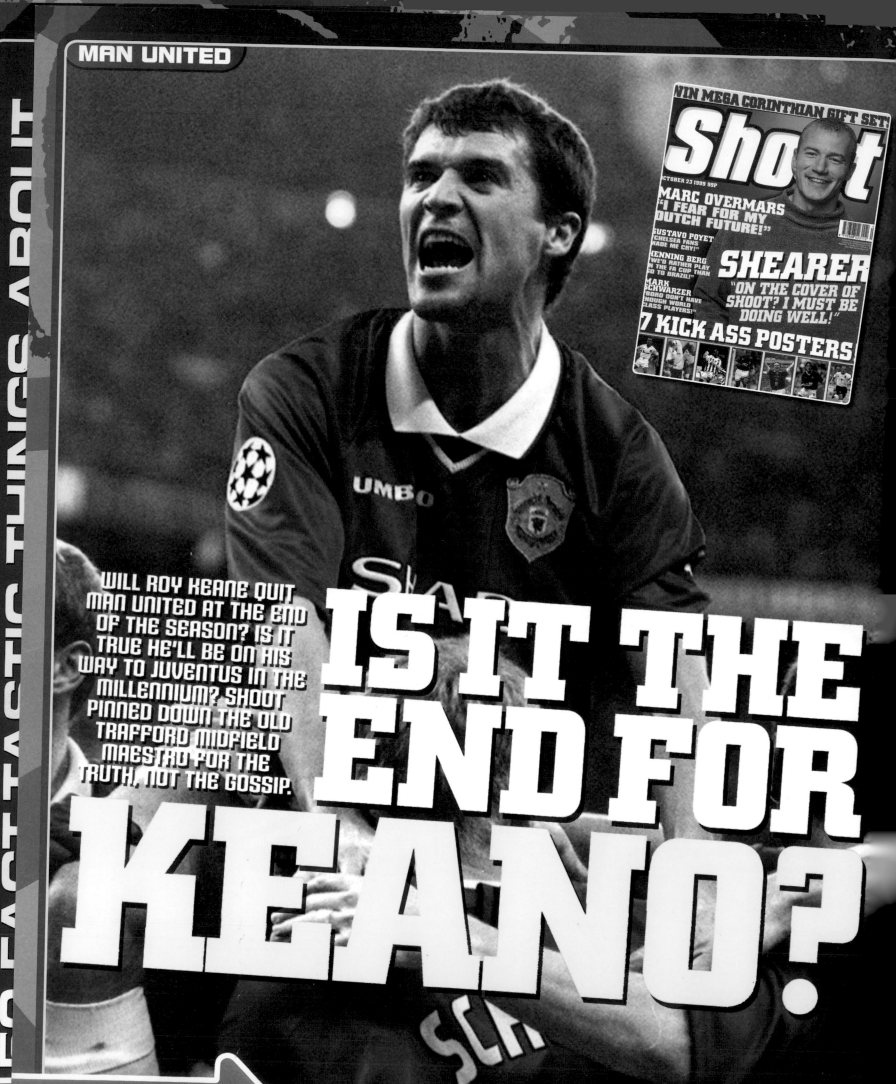

WILL ROY KEANE QUIT MAN UNITED AT THE END OF THE SEASON? IS IT TRUE HE'LL BE ON HIS WAY TO JUVENTUS IN THE MILLENNIUM? SHOOT PINNED DOWN THE OLD TRAFFORD MIDFIELD MAESTRO FOR THE TRUTH, NOT THE GOSSIP.

IS IT THE END FOR KEANO?

HOW IMPORTANT WAS IT TO WIN YOUR CHAMPIONS LEAGUE GROUP?

"Very. We knew we had to be seeded and the only way to do that was by winning our group. That was our one and only priority and despite a few disappointing performances along the way, we've achieved that so we're happy."

YOU'VE RECEIVED SOME STICK IN EUROPE, HAVEN'T YOU?

"The home games we've played so far have definitely been a bit of a disappointment and we've had to grind out the results. We have to raise ourselves an extra level for the next set of group games, that's for sure. Maybe some of the intensity hasn't been there and I think part of that is down to the change in format, with two teams going through. If you lost a game this season you still had a chance to qualify, whereas in the past, the tension has been on for you to win at all costs. If you lost a game you were struggling to go through at all."

SO WE'RE ABOUT TO SEE A LEANER, MEANER UNITED IN EUROPE FROM NOW ON THEN?

"The fans will be looking forward to seeing the bigger teams and we're no different. I think, like us, they've found it hard to get going when we were up against the likes of Croatia Zagreb and also Sturm Graz. No disrespect to the rest of the teams we've played, but we're in with the big boys now and we'll wind it up when the so-called bigger teams come along. Mind you, I suppose we're glad to avoid the likes of Barcelona and Lazio at the moment, but I'll bet they're glad they avoided us too. We don't fear anyone and like I said, I think you'll see a different United now that things have hotted up."

"I LOVE UNITED BUT I WON'T BE SELLING MYSELF SHORT."

Man United fans will be biting their finger nails down to the bone these next few months. Not just because United are going for the Premiership and European double but because Roy Keane could well be on his way out of Old Trafford.

The undisputed king of the United midfield has failed to sign a new contract and rumour has it that he's off to Juventus in the summer in return for some serious amounts of cash.

United know they have to come up with the readies to keep Keano but, in the meantime, the main man just wants to help the club to even more silverware.

"At the moment, all I'm interested in is seeing Man United stay at the top of the table and challenging in Europe," he told SHOOT. "I'm playing for the current treble winners and everyone is desperate to beat us. But I'm a determined character and a winner and I want to make sure we have another successful season before I decide my next move."

LET'S NOT BEAT AROUND THE BUSH, KEANO. WILL YOU QUIT UNITED AT THE END OF THIS SEASON?

"As much as I love Manchester United I am not going to sell myself short. I respect the club's position but they have to respect my position as well. As from January 1 other clubs have the chance to put a package together and then it will come back to United to see whether they can move towards what some of the other clubs can offer me, and we will have to take it from there."

IS UNITED'S UNWILLINGNESS TO PAY BIG WAGES STOPPING YOU FROM SIGNING THE BIG STARS?

"Yes, I would agree with that. United could have bought some good players down the years but they wouldn't come because of the wage structure."

YOU'VE WON THE TREBLE, SO IS IT HARD TO RAISE YOUR GAME AGAINST BRADFORD AND WATFORD?

"Not at all. All games are big games with Manchester United, whoever we are playing. I would rather be playing in big games all the time than Mickey Mouse ones for other clubs. That's what being a footballer is all about – it's a short career, so you might as well enjoy it while you can. I'm up for every game I play in, whether it's Bradford, Watford or Arsenal."

YOUR SHOUT

IS ROY KEANE ON HIS WAY? AND IF SO, TO WHERE? WE SPOKE TO SOME SHOOT READERS TO FIND OUT WHAT THEY THOUGHT.

It is time for Roy to move on and experience life in a different club and country.
Joe Ewamoh, 15, Elephant and Castle

United will offer enough money. Also Keane has a loyalty towards the club.
Adil Hafidi, 15, Blackfriars

Keane is getting greedy and I'm sure this will annoy Fergie. He's going.
James Murphy, 8, Waterloo

He is happy at Manchester United. They are the best club in the world. Why leave?
Adrian Palmer, 8, Wandsworth

If they win the Champions League again, he'll stay. Why move if there is no better club?
Shahin Samad, 12, Elephant and Castle

He's been there for ages and now it is time for Keane to move to Italy for a new challenge. He'll do really well out there.
Lolu Newton, 9, Vauxhall

Write to Redders!

It's the fab SHOOT Letters Page with the Liverpool and England star...

JAMIE REDKNAPP

> MY POSTMAN HAS BEEN DOIN' HIS NUT THIS WEEK, STRUGGLING THROUGH THE SNOW WITH ALL YOUR MAIL – I LOVE IT – JUST KEEP IT COMIN'

WRITE TO REDDERS SHOOT

Jamie's Top tips

Jamie, can you help me with some advice on passing? I've watched you for years now and love the way you spray the ball about, but I can't seem to get any distance or accuracy with my passes. Is there anything I can do?

Tim Forrest, aged 12 of Hykeham, Lincoln

JAMIE: Well, the best thing to try to do is get a playing surface to yourself, put some hoops down on the pitch and practice hitting the ball high into them. It does help if there's two of you as the other person can kick the ball back to you. Start with a short distance and then keep moving the hoops further back as you get better.

Teams, teams, teams...

Where are you? I haven't given out my Team of the Week award this week... 'cos there weren't any! So get yourselves sorted and send those team pics in with any decent stories...don't let me have to tell you again.

Is it true you have had a bust-up with Roy Evans about not playing in the first team?

Alan Smith from Welwyn Garden City

JAMIE: Never believe anything you read in the papers Alan. I have spoken to the gaffer but it's like everything at a big club like Liverpool, you have to wait for your chance and I've been assured I'm still part of the plans. It's up to me to shake off this injury and get back.

What do you think about Kevin Keegan's resignation?

Phil Thomas of Bury

JAMIE: Well, it was a big shock to everyone but there's a lot of pressure with a managerial job. Perhaps he felt it was time to give someone else a go but I think the Newcastle fans were always behind him no matter what. It's a shame he has gone but these things happen in football.

Can you tell me what you think about the golden goal rule they now use in top competitions like the European Championship?

Lisa McNeill of Aberdeen

JAMIE: I can tell you what...it's really nerve-wracking. I was so nervous when we played Germany in the Semi-Final of that competition and the strange thing about it is that once someone scores you don't get another chance to come back. It's exciting I suppose but it can't be good for the heart. It certainly wasn't for mine!

HERE'S HOW YOU CAN REACH ME

1 Send your letters to the address at the bottom of the page
2 Send me an E-mail on 106001.1105@Compuserve.com
3 Phone a special telephone hotline on 0891 137133 where you will be given 30 seconds to leave your question. Calls cost 45p per minute (cheap rate) and 50p per minute at all other times. Please make sure you have your parents' permission first.

REMEMBER...to keep sending in your photos and pix of your team. I love to get them and I'm having a ball answering them. See ya soon.

Redders' letter of the week

is from Alan Thompson of Ilford, Essex

Do you think that there should be a Super League involving Rangers and Celtic and clubs from abroad.

JAMIE: Good question, but I'm not sure the world's governing body FIFA would allow it to happen. A British League would mean that FIFA would count Scotland and England as one team on the international front and they wouldn't like that to happen north of the border.

Alan wins a pair of Jamie's Mizuno Premier S.I. boots

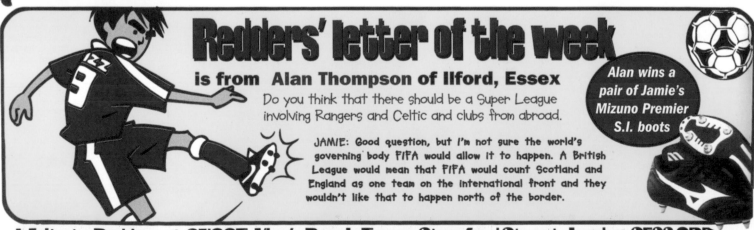

Write to Redders at SHOOT, King's Reach Tower, Stamford Street, London. SE99 OBB

TOP BOYZ
JAMIE CARRAGHER

We unearth the new names you're gonna be chanting before your burger's cold...

Who is he? Liverpool's hero last week against Aston Villa.

Where is he from? Bootle, in Liverpool - as if you couldn't tell from his interview on Match of the Day.

What's he like? A tall and slim ball player who does the holding role in the centre of the park.

When was he born? 28th January 1978, so it's his 19th birthday this Tuesday. But he's had his birthday present early - a Premiershi[goal.

Is he an international? Not quite. He missed out on the schoolboys and youth team but his performances this season have got him into the England Under-19 squad and he's hoping to make his international bow in a friendly before July's Under-20 World Finals in Malaysia. He's joined in the squad by fellow Reds Jamie Cassidy and David Thompson, both of whom have starred in SHOOT's Top Boyz this season.

Any other claims to fame? He played in last season's FA Youth Cup Final, when Liverpool beat West Ham home and away. It was Jamie's first experience of big crowds.

Has he played yet for Liverpool? Yep. He came on as a late sub in the Coca-Cola Cup defeat at Middlesbrough and played all of the second-half three days later, ironically at home to West Ham again, which ended 0-0. Then came the big one against Villa. In from the start alongside Jamie Redknapp because John Barnes and Michael Thomas where both out injured, he put in a compact performance and topped it all with the header that broke the deadlock and set the Reds on their way to a vital three points.

How highly rated is he? Very. He's the third teenager to come through Steve Heighway's youth system into the first team and Michael Owen is expected next. Roy Evans knows that his group of talented kids are as good as those Alex Ferguson introduced two years ago at Man United. Whether they'll bring home the trophies in 1999 is the question.

SHOOT RATING 8/10

Ritchie's chillin' out on the sofa but what is The Owls striker watching on the box?

Telly Addicts
...with Sheffield Wednesday's Ritchie Humphreys

Shooting Stars (BBC 2)
I love this. My favourite bit is the pub singer. I guess what song it is quite often. It's quite a favourite here actually where someone's got to get up and do a song in the pub style! Matt Clarke's actually got the Shooting Stars Pub Singer CD!

TFI Friday (Channel 4)
No, we don't watch the late showing - we're safely tucked up in bed by then, of course! I think Chris Evans is really good and he has some great guests on. He just has the bands on that he likes. Top stuff.

Harry Enfield and Chums (BBC1)
I like a lot of comedy programmes but this is excellent. Have you seen the new series? My favourite character is Julio Georgio, the new football signing. Paul Whitehouse is Julio, a Colombian who plays for Newcastle and he does this interview: "Hablo pablo liblia son catcho ron good ball from Beardo, like!"It's a classic.

Friends (Channel 4)
Another part of our essential Friday night pre-match viewing. It's fantastic. I fancy Rachel the most. Mind you, I think everyone does.

Only Fools and Horses (BBC 1)
You can't beat it. Did you see it at Christmas? I just loved the bit with Trigger when he won the medal. 'This is a photo of me with the mayor. That's me there.' Everyone was talking about it. I can't believe that they won't be making any more.

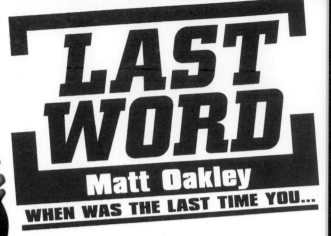

LAST WORD

Matt Oakley

WHEN WAS THE LAST TIME YOU...

BOUGHT A CAR?

"I recently bought an Aston Martin DB7 and it's really nice. I had owned a BMW before that but I'm happy with the car I have now. I've got a nice sound system in it as well, so you know when I'm about to turn up for training!"

PLAYED ANOTHER SPORT?

"Last week. I played a round of golf with my Saints team-mate Gary Monk. I play off a handicap of 16 at the minute, so I'm known to shank the odd shot or three. But when I play regularly and put my mind to it, I've been down to about nine or ten."

FELL ABOUT LAUGHING?

"David Hirst is really funny and he is the joker of the club. There's not too many practical jokes go on, it's more one-liners. But Hirsty is the main one for that and he can have you in stitches."

FELT REALLY PROUD?

"Representing England at under-21 level. I remember playing against Georgia at Charlton's ground and all my family turned up. When the National Anthem was played it brought a lump to my throat and it's made me determined to try and make the next step up at some point in the future."

BOUGHT A PRESENT FOR SOMEONE?

"I bought some clothes for my sister the other week. She'd seen the new Gap adverts and she liked the gear in them so I bought her back a few bits. I get a buzz when I go shopping and I like going to Bond Street in London."

WENT ON HOLIDAY?

"I went to America and Cyprus this summer, both times with my sister. We're very close, like best mates. She moved to Southampton about a year ago and we share a pad now."

COOKED A MEAL?

"Last week I cooked a nice pasta dish. I live with my sister and she looks after me well. She does most of the shopping but I don't mind doing some cooking. I'm not too bad, although it can be difficult as she's a vegetarian."

SCORED A GOOD GOAL?

"I was pleased with my effort the other week against Derby down at The Dell. I took the ball past a couple of defenders before tucking the ball wide of their 'keeper. There's no better thrill than scoring a goal and I've been hitting the target more often this season."

LEICESTER

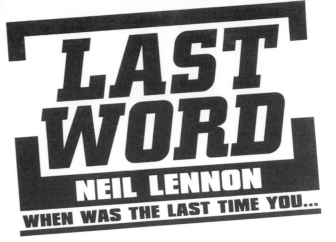

LAST WORD
NEIL LENNON
WHEN WAS THE LAST TIME YOU...

CALLED SOMEONE ON YOUR MOBILE PHONE?
"It was today actually when I gave my girlfriend a quick ring to say 'Hi!'. Sorry I couldn't say anything more exciting!"

LOST IT DURING A GAME?
"When we beat Sheffield Wednesday 3-0. Wim Jonk caught me with a late challenge which I was not pleased with. But I didn't retaliate as it wasn't intentional."

WERE MISTAKEN FOR SOMEONE ELSE?
"It has only happened once and it was during the time I dyed my hair blonde. A website company ran a feature of lookalikes where they claimed I was a dead ringer for Paul Newman. As if!"

SWAPPED SHIRTS WITH AN OPPONENT?
"Roy Keane kindly gave me his shirt after we played United the other week. But the last time I actually swapped mine was for Northern Ireland against Finland when I managed to get the shirt of their star player Jari Litmanen."

DID A LIVE TELEVISION INTERVIEW?
"It wasn't live but I was on Football Focus the other week being interviewed by Mark Bright playing snooker in the Willie Thorne snooker club."

COMPLAINED YOUR BOOTS WERE NOT BEING CLEANED PROPERLY?
"I had to have a quiet word with the young lad who cleans my boots a couple of weeks ago. Usually he does quite a good job but on this occasion he totally forgot. But I've already forgiven him and he'll get his Christmas tip – just as long as he doesn't do it again."

FELT REALLY NERVOUS BEFORE A GAME?
"I still get nervous before every game and I'm glad I do as it does give you a bit of fire in your belly for the start of the match. I suppose I'm more nervous when I go to places like Old Trafford but it's not as if I spend hours in the bog beforehand worrying!"

WATCHED AN OLD VIDEO OF YOURSELF IN ACTION?
"It was about four or five weeks ago when I was bored on a Friday afternoon. The game I watched was a memorable, but very frustrating one, when a couple of dodgy refereeing decisions saw us lose to Atletico Madrid in the Cup Winners' Cup a few years ago."

PLAYED A MUSICAL INSTRUMENT?
"I don't know about playing it but I messed around with a guitar the other week. Frank Sinclair can play the drums and I'd like to play the guitar alongside him one day. But as the lads will tell you from the karaoke nights, I'm more of a singer!"

NOT ALL ARSENAL PLAYERS DRESS LIKE MARTIN KEOWN. TAKE FREDDIE LJUNGBERG. THE SPIKEY ONE SPOKE TO SHOOT ABOUT FASHION AS WELL AS FOOTIE.

FREDDIE'S IN FASHION

Forget about David Beckham, there's a new style guru in town and he goes by the name of Freddie Ljungberg. OK, he might not be spotted in Milan at a Versace catwalk bash or eat at The Ivy, wearing the latest Vivienne Westwood, but have you seen the Arsenal midfielder's hair?!

Spikey is cool. Bleached red is even cooler. It's a combination which stands him out from the crowd and leaves Becks' blond highlights and goatee well in the shade.

Not that you'll ever find the super Swede having a go at Posh's other half.

"I like a lot of the clothes I see Beckham in," says Fred. "Like me, he obviously likes to look good. OK, he wears bandanas and a sarong but good luck to him. Why should he be told what he can and can't wear?"

Ljungberg also admires Beckham for what he's achieved at Man United but he doesn't feel The Gunners are too far behind their arch rivals.

"Man United won everything last season but we were only a point behind in the League and could have knocked them out of the FA Cup. But we are a much stronger side this season and we are determined to win back those trophies again."

SO WHAT'S WITH THE CRAZY, SPIKED LOOK?

"It's a pretty normal haircut back home in Sweden but I do get quite a lot of stick about it in the Arsenal dressing room, especially when I dyed it red, but I know the lads are only joking. I look different here but when I meet up with the Sweden squad, no-one mentions it at all."

YOU ALWAYS LOOK THE BEST DRESSED PLAYER AT ARSENAL.

"That's nice of you to say, but you'd never think so, judging by what I've got on today! I don't think I'm the best dressed player at the club because quite a few of the boys take a keen interest in fashion. Take Emmanuel Petit, he's even a part-owner of a boutique in London."

BUT YOU MUST BE INTO FASHION!

"Yes, I love buying clothes. As a footballer, I have quite a lot of spare time so I usually head to Bond Street or Marylebone to spend some of my money. I don't just buy labels though. I try to buy stuff that suits me"

STYLE FILE!

SO WHO ARE THE FLASHEST DRESSERS IN THE PREM? HERE'S SHOOT'S GUIDE TO TOP-FLIGHT STYLE GURUS.

(1) DAVID BECKHAM

The undisputed King Of Fash. Sarongs, shades, sandals. He does the lot!

(2) FREDDIE LJUNGBERG

Not a fan of combats, but the casual king. A lover of baggy jeans, apparently!

(3) DAVID JAMES

A real labels man and a former Armani model. Can't get much cooler than that.

(4) JAMIE REDKNAPP

Anyone who's got a fit babe like Louise as a wife has to look his best. Can't have the missus stealing the limelight you know!

(5) LES FERDINAND

Mr Sophistication. A fan of Hugo Boss from head to toe – black jumper right down to black brogues.

(6) DAVID GINOLA

Loves wearing Cerrutti gear but makes our top ten for his hair. How many blokes with grey hair can look that cool?

(7) ROBERTO DI MATTEO

We had to get one Italian in our top ten. Apparently he goes home to Rome just to do his shopping! And no, we don't mean Marks and Spencer!

(8) KEITH O'NEILL

A suits man but falls down our list as he was once spotted wearing shiny leather pants. Not cool at all.

(9) LEE SHARPE

Five years ago, Sharpey would have been No. 1 but he's fallen out of the limelight since he joined Bradford. Still, his spikey bleached looks are cool. But not as cool as Freddie's!

(10) ROBBIE SAVAGE

The loudest suits in the Midlands but lets himself down by having an Armani tattoo. How sad is that?

Southampton

THE SAINT GOES MARCHING ON

Life wasn't the same last season without **Matt Le Tissier** strutting his stuff at The Dell. He won't be there again this term either – but he does hope to be back to his best at Southampton's new ground! **Words: Colin Mitchell**

BIG THINGS are happening in Southampton, not least the development of the football club's new 30,000 seat St. Mary's stadium.

Nip down the road and you've got the giant West Quay shopping centre and hugely impressive retail park. But both of them are small fry when it comes to the biggest thing of all in the South Coast city.

We're talking about the man known as "Le God". No disrespect to former Saints players like Terry Paine, Mick Channon, Alan Ball and Kevin Keegan but Matt Le Tissier is now a legendary part of the club's history.

He has been with the club for an amazing 15 years – but that's not the end of the story. The Le Tissier book has another chapter to run as he has just signed a new one-year contract.

The gates may have closed for the last time at The Dell, but Matt left his mark there by scoring the final goal on the hallowed turf, in the 3-2 final day of the season win against Arsenal.

Now, his big aim is to notch up another piece of history by being the first player to score at the new ground when Southampton meet Espanyol of Spain in a pre-season friendly.

But first, back to the shopping centre, just days after the players went back into full training for the new campaign. Matt, along with a number of other squad members, was at West Quay to promote the team's new home and away shirts.

Fittingly, Matt descended from the skies for the occasion. He and his team-mates took over a glass-sided lift to lower them to the main shopping concourse.

"It's HIM! Look, up there." The woman in the white top and black skirt next to me was fast off the mark. She

pointed to the heavens as Le God was lowered to the stage area.

The loudspeakers counted down the seconds before the players, youth team members and even some of the ladies side eventually took to the catwalk.

First up was new signing Anders Svensson, who got a big cheer from the crowd. "I like playing up front, I am 25 and single," said the Swede of few words in pigeon English, his last comment presumably aimed at the local girls in the crowd.

Matt Oakley and James Beattie – sporting a somewhat dubious cropped blond haircut – also had the crowd putting their hands together in appreciation. The arrival of Dean Richards saw the rather large supporter in The Saints' red and white striped shirt jump

It's a long time since we've had such a strong squad at the club.

onto the bench near me. "Deano, Deano, Deano…" There's no doubt that the reliable defender is now also a popular player in Hampshire.

Then the big moment arrived. The announcer said what we all knew anyway. "The next item of clothing is modelled by a man who, I am sure, will get a big welcome." Of course he will you fool! Don't you realise who it is?

Enter from the back of the catwalk, through a plume of dry ice, Matt Le Tissier, giant smile from ear to ear and right arm held aloft in that familiar goal celebration gesture.

Our man in the red and white shirt had now turned into Mr Blobby – an over-excited sea of limbs and squeals. He was almost overcome that his biggest hero was just feet away. Both arms outstretched, the top half of his body and his head bowed in salute to the King of the Solent.

He might not be the greatest model in the world, but Matt swept down the stage, outstretched his arms and gave us all a twirl. He'd arrived, he'd done his stuff, he had conquered. So Matt, was it harder to take a step down the catwalk than take to the pitch?

"Not at all, it was great fun, I loved it, it was easier than playing a game," said the great man, still grinning like the proverbial Cheshire cat.

And smile he might. He's a folk hero in these parts, especially after scoring *that* final goal at The Dell.

"It meant a hell of a lot to me. I couldn't have asked for a better finish at the ground," the smile had slipped just slightly from Matt's face. He'd got serious. You could see just how much that goal really meant.

"It was all I had hoped for from the game, without any doubt. I had thought about it the week before – now I would →

Southampton

→ like to get the first one at the new ground, I'd love to."

So, what odds on you scoring that one Matt? "You'll have to ask the manager whether he is going to pick me or not. You just never know." The smile and a laugh are back.

"I'm a little bit sad, of course, that we are leaving The Dell. But we had to have a new stadium and I am sure that we will make good use of it. We aren't even allowed onto the turf until about August 9, but I am looking forward to it."

It's yet another season on the club's books, in an era when football stars sometimes change clubs almost as often as their socks. Matt has taken criticism for his loyalty. Accusations of lacking ambition and settling for the easy life are two easy taunts.

But Matt has always loved life on the South Coast, and the new contract was a real bonus after last season's injury-ridden campaign.

"The contract will take me until I am 33, nearly 34, so it may not be too long after that, we'll just have to wait and see how it goes. I may get another year after that, who knows? It all depends on how the body feels, if I can keep clear of injuries and my body keeps allowing me to perform at this level.

"All of my injury problems feel as though they are okay at the moment and during the summer I took a complete break. I didn't do anything stupid so I could steer clear of all possible injuries."

When we caught up with Matt he was less than a week into full training, just before the club went off to La Manga to step up their fitness regime even further. So how had it all gone so far? "It's been okay, although today was a bit tough."

New ground, new contract and a new manager. "Yes, Stuart Gray took over temporarily at the end of last season so we know what he is all about and I am sure the lads will respond to him."

Saints, mostly under Glenn Hoddle, played exceptionally well last term but a poor run-in after the old manager left saw them fall out of contention for a place in Europe – although tenth in the Premiership was no disgrace.

For most of that time Matt was out of the picture, struggling with injury. One can only speculate about what could have happened if he had squeezed in a few more matches.

"It was only the last three or four games that I was on the bench. It was

New men on the block

New manager **STUART GRAY** (right) is 41 and signed for Nottingham Forest as a player in 1980.

He spent just over two years at Forest, working under the legendary Brian Clough before going on loan to Bolton.

In 1983 the midfielder/defender moved to Barnsley where he made 117 appearances between 1983-87, scoring 27 goals.

Aston Villa manager Graham Taylor bought Stuart for £150,000 in 1987. He spent three years there before moving to Saints in 1991.

Injury cut his career short after just ten appearances and he moved to Wolves as reserve team coach.

He returned to Southampton to work in the community coaching department and later manager Dave Jones made him reserve team coach, before stepping up to the first team coach role.

He retained the job under Glenn Hoddle, was handed the caretaker manager's reins in March, and became manager three months later.

Forward **ANDERS SVENSSON**, 25, a Swedish international, has signed on a four-year contract from Elfsborg. He cost Southampton around £750,000 and is likely to play as an attacking midfielder, or just behind the main strikers.

He ended his career in Sweden by scoring the winning goal from 30 yards against rivals Gothenburg, earning him a standing ovation.

Republic of Ireland wing-back **RORY DELAP** has also signed for a club record £4m from Derby

nice to get on a couple of times and finish as we did, beating Arsenal and Man United in the last week.

"It was very frustrating. I am bad at sitting out games, even when we are winning. But when we are not picking up points I am even worse."

Southampton have produced a number of stars over the years, a crop of flair players who have attracted attention and even received international call-ups. But, with the exception of their FA Cup win in1976, arguably they remain a bit of a bridesmaid side. Things could be changing.

"Anders has come in, which is good, and the chairman has said there's the chance of a couple more so we are building a strong squad.

"I think times are looking really bright for Southampton. It is a long time since we have had a squad as strong as this so, hopefully, we can improve on what we did last season.

"We want a top ten finish, that's a realistic aim. That would be a fantastic improvement on last year," admitted Southampton's most loyal servant.

Mr Blobby would probably agree. But you'd probably have to scrape him off the roof of the West Quay if Saints go higher than tenth or win anything.

Top right: Matt struts his stuff in the new away kit during the West Quay fashion show.
Above and right: Matt and his Southampton team-mates take to the catwalk to show off home and away kits. Note: both have the same shorts.
Below left: Saints fans will be hoping to see more of Matt in action this season.

Golden guy

Knighted in the Queen's Golden Jubilee year, Bobby Robson still can't see an end to his 50-plus years in football, despite hitting 70 next February.

EXCLUSIVE WORDS: Colin Mitchell

THE BIG INTERVIEW

THERE'S ONLY ONE BOBBY ROBSON. And the good news for Newcastle United fans is that he has yet to decide when he is going to blow the final whistle on his time in football.

There has been speculation that The Magpies boss, with more than 50 years in the beautiful game under his belt, would quit at the end of next season.

But in an exclusive interview with *Shoot Monthly* Bobby said: "My gut reaction is to keep on working, to do what I want to do.

"I realise how old I am - but age is just a number. I feel great, I am happy, I am with a great club and I love to work. I know people will be thinking what an old goat he is...that's

I KNOW PEOPLE WILL BE THINKING WHAT AN GOAT HE IS BUT THAT'S NOT NEW

nothing new. But as long as my health is good, I am doing what I want to do and as long as I am successful I will carry on.

"The day our results go... people will say it is time for him to go and I understand that."

Another suggestion has been that Bobby will elect to move upstairs at St. James' Park, possibly in a director football role, should he put some silverware in the cabinet during the coming season.

But he told us: "Winning or losing some silverware wouldn't affect my decision, to be honest. That's a good position to retire if you win something, isn't it? But I might want to improve on that.

"So winning something for Newcastle next year wouldn't determine my position," he added.

So would he consider a move upstairs? "I don't think so. That will be it. That's why I want to keep working because I don't know what I will do with myself.

"I don't want to go shopping on Saturday afternoons, I don't want to have extended holidays, I don't want to play golf all of the time. I have a nice, balanced life but the bulk of my life is football, I am in love with it.

"People ask why I keep carrying on, but the answer is because I adore it, I need it. What would I do without football? I don't know, it would be a bit of a blow I would have thought. As long as my health is good and my motivation is high I will keep at it."

Bobby is everyone's favourite grandad, the man you trust, the leader you admire, the manager who can bring you success. Everywhere he has gone the genial Geordie has picked up trophies, from his early days at Ipswich, through stints in Portugal, Holland and Spain, where he led the mighty Barcelona to a lorry load of silverware.

But, so far, he has yet to crack the 33-year barren spell at his beloved Newcastle United. It was way back in 1969 that The Magpies carried off the old Inter City Fairs Cup under the late Joe Harvey.

As the man who transformed the club from the deadmen of the Premiership into Champions League contenders, all in under three years, Bobby is only too aware of what picking up a trophy would mean to the fans.

"It would be Utopia, the city would just be swimming in emotion if we did bring something home. And that is our intention," said Bobby.

"I know the public, and euphoria would set in. We have got an amazing support up there and a nice stadium and we have supporters to match the stadium. We just have to give them what they deserve."

In fact, after collecting trophies all around Europe, Bobby admits that winning with Newcastle would be the icing on what has been an incredible career.

"Well, yes it would. I have won things abroad in all the places I have been to, I did the same at Ipswich where we won the FA Cup and the UEFA Cup and we got close to success with England. Getting to the semi-final of the World Cup 12 years ago was no mean feat.

"But this is my last job. I won't go anywhere else from here. If I can finish on a silver note - not so much for me because I have won things - it would be great for the club and the public. It's what is needed."

Young at heart

ALL OF HIS PLAYERS praise him, his results speak for themselves, so what is the secret of Bobby Robson's success? The simple answer has to be his desire to stay young at heart.

"I am out on the pitch every day with the players because I like it. One of the things I like about my job is that I am working with young players all of the time.

"I am not a manager who can sit upstairs drinking coffee and making decisions. I couldn't do that. The moment I don't want to be on the pitch with the players every morning is the day I say it is time I went.

"That is my forte, that's what I like. Working out with young players keeps you bright, keeps you young. The players keep me bright, keep me sharp, keep me alert."

He's also something of a rarity in these days of players and managers changing clubs at the drop of a hat or a big fat cheque.

A few years *before* he actually moved to his native North East to take over at Gallowgate, Bobby had been wanted by the Newcastle board as manager.

Despite the huge tugs on his heart strings that longed for a return to his native part of the country, and a team he supported as a boy, Bobby decided to stay loyal to Barcelona. He had just signed a new contract.

But unknown to Bobby, the Barca hierarchy had already signed a deal to bring in Dutch coach Louis van Gaal as his successor and decided to move our favourite Geordie upstairs.

"I finished second in the league by two points, we won the European Cup Winners Cup, the Spanish Cup, the Super Cup - but they didn't know how well I was going to do. They had already signed him on a hidden contract which I didn't know about. They didn't know I would do so well.

"If I had known this, and that there would be a big problem at the club, I would have said hold on, if that is what you are going to do I am going, I am leaving.

"They honoured my contract financially but they didn't honour my position."

However, the Newcastle job had already been turned down and Bobby admits that he regrets missing out on that opportunity.

"But at the time I was in the middle of a marvellous football season, I had waited 18 years to get to Barcelona and I wasn't in a hurry to leave. When the Newcastle offer came it was very difficult for me. I felt that I had to honour my contract.

"There was a special clause in my contract that said if I left during it I would have to pay back double what they paid me.

"I knew that, I didn't have a problem with it, I didn't go there to walk out, I went there to work, so I was happy with that clause," he added.

Japanese year of the underdog

END OF THE FOOTBALL SEASON, and a time to relax before the next pressure-cooker atmosphere of the Premiership. But not if you are a football-obsessed Bobby Robson.

Instead, it's a trip to the television studios to watch the World Cup and be an expert summariser for ITV.

As a former England manager, he is better qualified than most to give his views on the game and he reckons the England national team did us proud in Japan and Korea.

"Full credit to them We did well to qualify, we did well to get out of the Group of Death. Everyone thought that was going to be difficult but we made it, got five points and knocked out the team that were going to be a danger. That defeat by us of Argentina more or less skittled them home.

"We were not so good against Sweden, very good against Argentina not so good against Nigeria. I am glad we didn't have to beat them to quality, I tell you!

"One point was sufficient in that heat, and the heat was awful. Early afternoon with temperatures soaring is not easy to play in and that probably affected our performances.

"Our lads looked wilted, a little bit short of energy and I think the weather conditions were definitely working against us.

"They were good against Denmark and not so good against Brazil in the second half, although fairly good in the first. Their goal came at the worst possible time for us and the second goal, I still think, was something of a fluke and at another bad time."

Plain talking from a manager that all fans respect. They would probably agree with his views on just how far England could have gone.

"It was there for us to win. You could see this stepping stone situation, going from one to another to get to the other side of the river. But we didn't perform well enough in the second half against Brazil's ten players to come away with a victory.

"So we didn't deserve to win it when it was there for us, sadly. We know we had the greatest chance for some time, since '66, of winning it. We really did, we have never had such a great chance as that.

"A lot of the players will again be available and better, more experienced, more

THE WORLD CUP WAS THERE FOR US TO WIN. WE HAD THE BEST CHANCE SINCE '66.

knowledgeable, stronger, fitter... so the future is good. In between now and four years time we will find some more players coming through, we always do.

"You have to think about (Joe) Cole, how good he will be, Dyer will be better, Carrick might come in, Defoe, Carl Cort... I don't know, but in the next four years we will produce some players to add to the great ones we have already got."

PLANNING FOR THE FUTURE

YOU MIGHT EXPECT that the manager's main aim was to get much-needed trophies into the cabinet at Gallowgate, but being the forward-thinking person that he is, Bobby is planning much further ahead than that.

His big ambition is not only to win things, but also put the club on a great footing for the next generation, set them up for when he does, eventually, call it a day.

"I am laying the foundations for the future. That is how I see it. I want to leave the club in really good shape. I am buying good, young players, that is why I bought JJ (Jermaine Jenas) who is only 19," said Bobby.

Within the past few weeks he has also forked out more than £8m for another 19-year-old, Portugal international Hugo Viana from Sporting Lisbon.

"We finished fourth last season and had a wonderful year. Now we have bought a fine young player in Hugo, who I like very much

"He's a left-footed player, rare in this age of ours, who will give us a better balance. He is young, only 19, but is a big talent."

The plan is to play Viana on the left side of midfield as back up for the veteran Gary Speed, and support so that flying French winger Laurent Robert can get forward even more.

"There is one more player that we very much want to buy - when is this going out? (we tell him the date) By the time this is printed I hope you will find that we have bought another player, a central defender," revealed Bobby.

Don't bet against that player being Ipswich's Titus Bramble.

Of course players aren't the

only key element to the future success of a club, they also need a good coach or manager. The fans will tell you that Alan Shearer is destined to be the new boss. Bobby told us what is really happening behind the scenes.

"To be honest my successor hasn't really cropped up. There has been no vibes about that from anyone at the club, no-one is looking at that," revealed Bobby. But surely he has his own views on his eventual replacement?

"The future at Newcastle looks bright, but you can never guarantee it. I know how old I am but what I have to do is consider what is the next best step for Newcastle United and advise the board accordingly.

"Whether they take that on board or not I don't know but I need to look at that... what is

going to happen to the club after I've moved on."

So what does he specifically think of the Shearer for manager suggestions? "I haven't got a view on that and I think I should keep out of it.

"I don't know what he wants to do - but what I have told him to do is concentrate on giving us another two years.

"But I think over the next year I will have to give that whole scenario some thought so I can give the board some advice."

Bobby highlighted yet again the young age of his current crop of stars, including Craig Bellamy (22), Carl Cort (24), Aaron Hughes (22), Shola Ameobi (20) and his two 19-year-olds.

We pointed out, tongue in cheek, that Republic of Ireland goalkeeper Shay Given is something of a veteran at the grand old age of 26.

"But he has got eight good years left!" came back the reply quick as a flash.

Aside from the management issue, the big worry among fans though is what happens when the legendary Alan Shearer does hang his boots up. Who can replace the goal-scoring machine?

"That is why we are trying to develop Carl Cort and Shola up front, if they don't replace him then we will have to look again but we have a little bloke called Chopra coming though, Michael Chopra, who we love.

"So we have some candidates in the pipeline and if they don't come up to spec... the world is our oyster, but where do we find our golden nugget again? That's why we hope to produce our own."

Brazil double up on plucky Turks

BRAZIL 1 TURKEY 0

IF TURKEY NEEDED any added motivation to upset the Samba beat of the Brazilans they had only to reflect on the manner of their defeat to Ronaldo and and friends in the group stages of this competition.

Having matched their more illustrious opponents punch for punch, the Turks saw a well-earned point swiped away by an over-zealous referee and a hotly disputed penalty.

Add to the mix a piece of gamesmanship from Rivaldo, which not only resulted in Hakan Unsal's dismissal for kicking the ball at an opponent, but also suggested that the Barcelona star has a future in amateur dramatics – and you've got a heady mix.

In an open match, Turkey again proved that they have developed into a side with genuine international class and in the early stages looked the more accomplished outfit.

One surprise however, was the inclusion of the struggling Hakan Suker at the expense of Ilhan Mansiz who had scored the golden goal against Senegal.

Defensively, Brazil again appeared vulnerable but the constant threat of Rivaldo and Ronaldo (Ronaldinho was suspended) ensured that this game would not remain scoreless.

Sure enough, four minutes after half-time Ronaldo, now sporting a strange new hairstyle, conjured up a piece of individual magic.

Collecting the ball on the left, he ran at a static Turkish defence, glided into the area and ignoring the attentions of three opponents shot early with a good old-fashioned toe-poke. Despite a half-save from Rustu the ball ended up in the back of the net.

Edilson, put through by Ronaldo, was denied by a last-ditch tackle by Akyel as Brazil sought a

Right: Ronaldo - complete with new haircut - gives Turkey the runaround.

game-clinching second goal. With the game stretched, opportunities came thick and fast with both Brazilian fullbacks, Cafu and Carlos, marauding forward at every opportunity.

Ronaldo was substituted in the 68th minute as a precaution for his thigh injury but possibly also to remove him from an ongoing feud

with the Turkish defence. Six minutes later, Leicester's Muzzy Izzet made an appearance for his adopted country.

At the final whistle, Brazil celebrated their seventh World Cup appearance. Turkey, with their heads held high, could look back on a wonderful campaign.

Sweet and sour for Ballack

GERMANY 1 SOUTH KOREA 0

EVEN THE MOST HARDENED of footie cynics must have shed a silent tear when South Korea's exciting - and not uncontroversial - passage to the World Cup Final was derailed by those pesky Germans.

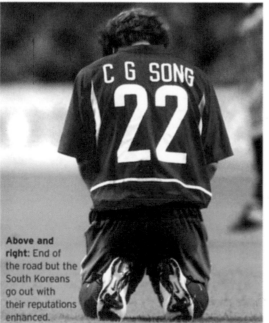

Above and right: End of the road but the South Koreans go out with their reputations enhanced.

Much was expected of Guus Hiddink's super-fit team, especially as Germany came into the game with the legendary Franz Beckenbauer's damning criticism ringing in their ears. Perversely, Germany responded to his taunts – something about throwing them all in a bag and giving it a bit of a wallop – and put in their best performance of the tournament.

South Korea, on the other hand, seemed slightly overawed by the occasion, possibly unnerved by the absence of key striker Ahn Jung-Hwan who failed to start through injury.

The first 15 minutes passed fairly uneventfully with Korea looking to play their pressure football while a solid looking German side concentrated on the counter-attack. The pace is fast, the football slick but the final ball remained disappointing. A powerful shot in the ninth minute from Lee Chun-Soo, excellently saved by Kahn, was the only real goal threat.

Half-time saw the scores level and after the break, Voller's instructions resulted in Ballack and Hamman taking more of a proactive role in midfield.

A defining moment came in the 72nd minute. South Korea broke forward with two men to spare but as Park Ji-Sing prepared to shoot on the edge of the box, Ballack committed a "professional" foul. His intervention snuffed out the co-host's best opportunity of the game but also meant that if Germany made the final, they would be without arguably their best player.

To add more misery upon South Korea, the culpable Ballack scored at the second attempt to send Germany through to play Brazil for the first time in a competitive match.

South Korea were out but not down as seven million people took to the streets to salute an effort that proved that David can indeed beat Goliath – and more than once!

Ronaldo runs riot

BRAZIL 2 GERMANY 0

YOU COULDN'T HAVE written a better script. First we had the Germans - tipped by most to make an early exit - defying all expectations to make it to the World Cup Final.

The wounds from that 5-1 mauling at the hands of the English and an undignified last-ditch qualification were still a bit raw. Clearly a win against Brazil in the 69, 000 Yokohama stadium would end such painful associations.

Then, we have the Brazilians. They too struggled to qualify and coach Phil Scolari was so unpopular back home that he was assaulted in the street. Yet, the biggest hurdle to overcome, was the memories of four years ago when they were beaten by France in the '98 Final. They too had a score to settle.

It would also be remiss to ignore the story of all stories: Ronaldo's comeback from physical and mental tortures. A strangely lacklustre showing in the last final and three years of injury problems, meant this occasion represented more than a game of football. It was an opportunity for Ronaldo to set the record straight.

In the run up to the match, much was made of the clash of styles between these two football superpowers. Brazil's flair against Germany's economy, delightful expression against form and functionality.

However, soon after referee Collina blew the start, it became clear that Rudi Voller's men were not content to were here for a game. Playing neat, flowing football from defence to midfield the industrious Germans were the better side. Jeremies - in for the suspended Ballack - and Liverpool's Hamann, superbly contained the threats of the Brazilian midfield, while launching wave after wave of counter-attacks. Unfortunately the final ball, allied with a lack of firepower up front, meant Brazil 'keeper Marcos had a fairly quiet 45 minutes.

Although it took a while for Scolari's men to gather some momentum, they showed enough in the opening period to suggest that they would open their account sooner rather than later. Midfielder Kleberson came close with a 20 yard shot which smacked the bar.

Ronaldo, who started the game with six goals and was in pole position to claim the golden boot, spurned three gilt-edge chances with only Kahn to beat.

The first, from a through ball by Ronaldhino, he fired inexplicably wide. The other two struck the body of the German 'keeper.

After the break, Germany again started stronger and almost scored with a Jeremies header.

Then came the moment on which the game eventually hinged. Early in the second-half, the impressive Neuville - scorer of only four goals in 35 internationals - lined up a free-kick from way outside the Brazilian box.

His shot screamed over the wall and seemed destined for the top corner, only for Marcos to launch himself at the last instant and tip the ball onto the post and away to safety.

Marcos later made an equally good save from substitute Bierhofff to make a lie of the notion that he was the weak link in an already fragile backline.

Germany's chances were effectively ended in the 67th minute. Ronaldo lost possession, only to outmuscle Hamann and feed his fellow partner in crime Rivaldo. The Barcelona star fired a snap shot that Kahn would normally have gathered with ease, but fumbled into the path of the onrushing Ronaldo who made no mistake. 1-0 Brazil.

It was an amazing error by the German stopper, voted the best goalkeeper in the tournament by FIFA just prior to the match.

If the first goal was scrappy, the second was an exhibition of Brazilian football. Eleven minutes later, a cross-field ball from the ever-adventurous Cafu was dummied by Rivaldo on the edge of the German area. With perfect touch, Ronaldo controlled and passed his shot into the corner of Khan's net. 2-0.

Ronaldo's eight goals secured the Golden

Left and far left: Brazil's biggest hero!
Bottom left: Ronaldo scores his second.
Bottom: He Kahn't believe it.

Boot but his total of 12 in the World Cup equalled the record of Pele.

The last ten minutes were like a training match with the game stretched and each side looking to score.

The final whistle went and the party really began. Voller sportingly sought out a tearful Ronaldo to express his congratulations, while Pele - grinning from ear to ear - contemplated yet another Brazilian triumph.

MAN OF THE MATCH

WHO ELSE? For strength of character and sheer footballing ability, Ronaldo deserves all the plaudits. His eight goals in the competition won him the Golden Boot but made him the first player for 28 years to score more than six goals in the finals.

FINAL FACTS

GERMANY: Kahn, Linke, Ramelow, Metzelder, Frings, Schneider, Jeremies (Asamoah 77), Hamann, Bode (Ziege 84), Neuville, Klose (Bierhoff 73). **Booked:** Klose.
BRAZIL: Marcos, Edmilson, Lucio, Roque Junior, Cafu, Kleberson, Gilberto, Carlos, Ronaldinho (Juninho 85), Rivaldo, Ronaldo (Denilson 90). **Booked:** Roque Junior.
ATTENDANCE: 69,029.
REFEREE: Pierluigi Collina (Italy).

BIG WITH BECKS

England skipper David Beckham may be a world-wide superstar in his own right - but check out who *he* thinks are living legends. **WORDS:** Colin Mitchell

HE'S ONE OF THE MOST FAMOUS footballers in the world, a fashion icon, admired by women, envied by men and with a lifestyle that can only be described as amazing.

David Beckham says that he can live with the pressures and the adulation that come with his massive global status... but he does have one startling admission.

The great man and England skipper is star-struck when it comes to meeting his own personal heroes!

Yes, the guy who can play in front of 60,000-plus Manchester United fans without a care in the world; who rode out a storm of hatred when he was sent off in the 1998 World Cup Finals; who coped admirably when he was restored to national hero for helping England qualify for last year's tournament in the Far East gets a touch of the shakes when he considers his heroes.

So just who are these amazing people? Other football celebs? Rock or pop stars? Glamorous models or actors? No, they are two widely different icons from generations before Becks was even a glint in his dad's eye.

Former world heavyweight boxing champion Muhammad Ali and old-time slapstick comedian Norman Wisdom - a man three times his age - are the midfielder's most admired stars.

"Yeah, I was quite nervous when I met Norman Wisdom, because I used to watch his programmes and his films as a youngster" admitted Becks.

"I have met quite a few people, but Muhammad Ali was one of the best I've met. Of course I get

star-struck because, you know, you look up to these people, they're famous," said David.

And David knows all about the fame game. Having lived in the public eye since his early teens and of course, being a half of one of the most high-profile couple on the planet, the 27-year-old has had a heavy burden to bear. So how does he cope with the adulation he receives from fans?

"I wouldn't say there's any bad things about being famous really, the attention comes with it. Sometimes it gets a little bit too much, but you've got to learn to handle that because it's part and parcel of being famous and being in a world-class football team.

"I get a little bit more than some other people but, that's part of my life now. I've learned to handle that," he added.

David also revealed when he first realised that he had really arrived in the eyes of United fans. "It was when I scored against Galatasaray in 1994 and the fans started singing 'There's only one David Beckham.' That was nice.

"Scoring the goal against Wimbledon (from the half-way line in 1996) and then going away on pre-season tour is when I started to realise that people knew me outside Manchester. That was also nice."

One of his other early memories about fame was when he won a Bobby Charlton Soccer Skills competition at the age of 11.

"I was in the local paper and a couple of tabloids, and people started showing a little bit of interest in me and saying that I was going to go to United because I had always been a fan."

And the trip to last year's World Cup? Presumably the fanatical support he personally received helped seal that world-wide superstar status?

"I'm not sure about that, but the reception over in Japan was certainly an experience that I've never enjoyed before. Hopefully it will now continue," David added.

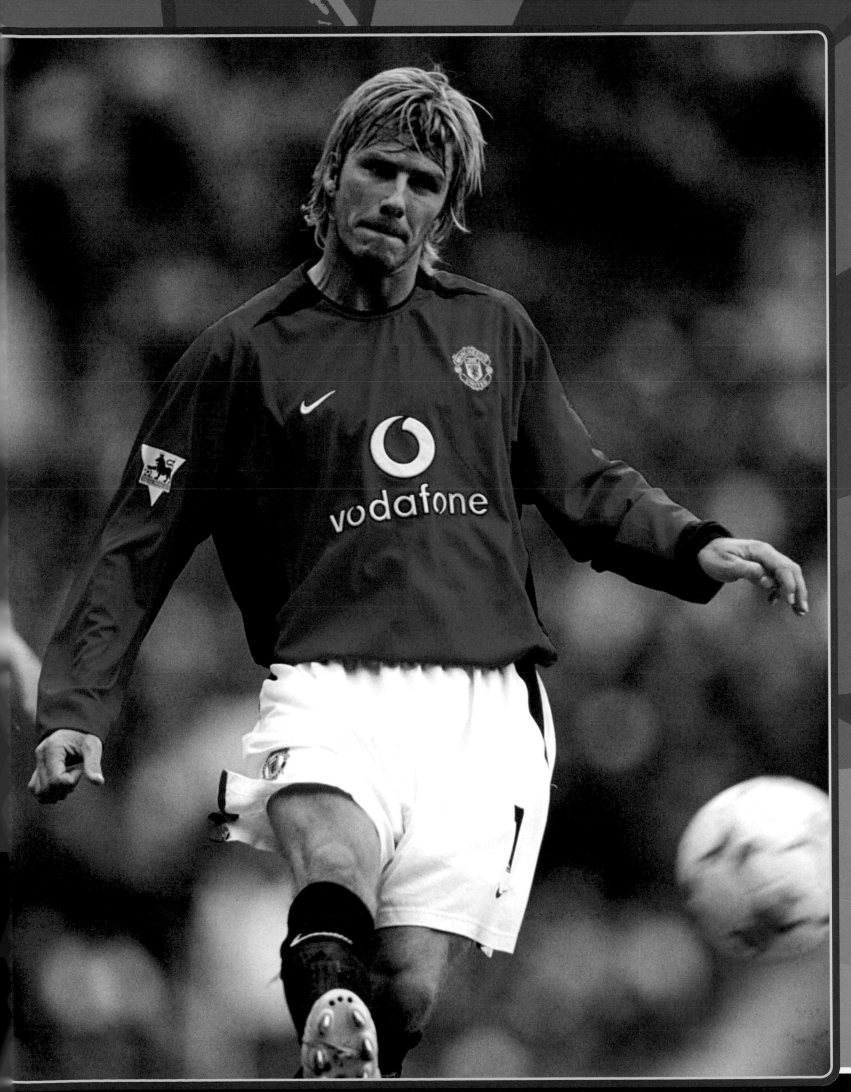

HOW TO BE A STAR

DAVID BECKHAM has a message for aspiring youngsters who are worried about failing to make the big-time - don't give up!

Becks is the man with everything, fame, money, pop star wife, nice homes and flash cars, he will admit that everything in his life hasn't been a fairytale.

"I've had knock-backs before. I wanted to get into the England Under-18s and Under-19s and never did that, because I was told I was too small," he recalled.

"For kids, getting knocked back sometimes is good because you go on from there and you push on and hopefully bounce back.

"I think that's what made United dump me, because I was really small the first time I went up to Manchester. I'm glad they saw something else than rather just looking at my size, because I shot up to 6ft 1in. It must be the air or something up there," he laughed.

But even if you are a mega-star there is something you must always remember, and that is you are part of a team

"I've realised that since joining Manchester United. If you get that bond between players then, you know, you can go on to great things and become a strong team," said David.

"Kids have just got to relax, go out there, enjoy themselves, play as a team but if there is a chance to do something special or be an individual then do it. But you have also got to think about your team-mates because it's not just about one player, it's about the whole team," he added.

"I'm lucky enough to do it at a club I've supported as a boy and the whole way through my life. To walk out at Old Trafford is a dream come true for me and it gets better every time you walk down that tunnel."

As well as respecting the team ethic David also appreciates that the growing body and mind needs constant attention.

He explained: "Rest is important. For instance when I'm in pre-season training I'll go home in the afternoon, I'll have a sleep, I'll try to relax.

"I'll eat well and I'll sleep well at night and you've got to keep drinking if it's hot as you can get a bit dehydrated. You've got to prepare off the pitch as well as on it."

And a few last words of advice: "Play hard and win big. The harder you train, the more you gain." ☻

WHO ARE THEY?

If you've never heard of them, here's all you need to know about Becks' heroes

MUHAMMAD ALI

ARGUABLY the greatest-ever heavyweight boxing champion Ali (right) was *the* showman - his self-proclaimed style summed up by the catchphrase: "floats like a butterfly, stings like a bee."

Born on January 17, 1942, in Louisville, Kentucky, as christened Cassius Clay, he began boxing at the age of 12 and before the end of a 21-year professional career became a hero for black America.

He had dazzled at amateur level, dominating the light-heavyweight scene and winning a gold medal at the Rome Olympics in 1960.

He won his first professional heavyweight title in 1964 at the age of 22 when he knocked out huge favourite Sonny Liston. Nine successful title defences followed.

Having joined the Black Muslim sect - when he renamed himself Muhammad Ali because Cassius Clay was a "slave name" - Ali became increasingly involved in the civil rights movement, sometimes with dramatic consequences. His ban from boxing for refusing to to join the US Army cost him three years of his career, and nearly resulted in a prison sentence.

His 1971 come-back against champion Joe Frazier saw a ring-rusty Ali beaten. He gained revenge two years later and defeated Smokin' Joe for the final time in "The Thrilla in Manilla" in 1975. However it was the previous year's "Rumble in the Jungle" in Zaire against George Foreman that remains the stuff of legend. In a brutal encounter Ali emerged triumphant at the age of 32 - only the second man ever to win back the title.

The end of Ali's career was painful to watch as he continued way beyond his peak. But in terms of boxing ability, charisma and sheer showmanship Muhammad Ali will always be "the greatest."

NORMAN WISDOM

THE ENGLISH-BORN slapstick comedian was starring on the stage as far back as 19... And, although difficult to believe, is still something of a national institution.

Even today his catchphrase of "Mr Grimsdale, Mr Grimsdale" is remembered by young and old, as are his ill-fitting suits and his cap, set at a jaunty angle.

Born on February 4, 1915, in London, Norman was awarded an OBE in 1995 and received a knighthood in 2000.

Curiously he became a cult figure in communist Albania where, during the Cold War, the country was cut off from the western world. For some strange reasons Norman Wisdom's comedy films were still accepted by their government as suitable for public viewing.

Becks actually got to meet his unlikely hero Sir Norman when England played in Albania in 2001 for a World Cup qualifier (below). The comedian took to the pitch and as the players warmed up for the game he managed to steal the show with a trademark stumble. Laugh? The team nearly cried!

Now and then

Shoot has been your best guide to football players for more than 30 years. Check out how time has altered the lifestyles, habits and tastes of stars past and present.

EVERTON

THEN: 1981

Full name: Stephen McMahon.
Birthplace: Liverpool.
Birthdate: August 20, 1961.
Height: 5ft 8in.
Weight: 11st 3lb.
Previous clubs: None.
Married: No.
Car: Renault 18TS.
Favourite newspaper: Daily Mail.
Favourite player: Diego Maradona.
Promising team-mates: Joe McBride and Kevin Ratcliffe.
Favourite other team: Aston Villa.
Football hero of childhood: Alan Ball.
Favourite other sport: I like all sports.
Most difficult opponent: The manager.
Most memorable match: Our FA Cup victory over Liverpool last season.
Biggest disappointment: Losing on my League debut at Sunderland.
Friendliest away fans: Most of them are friendly.
Favourite food-drink: Scampi and milk.

Miscellaneous likes and dislikes: Winning and picking up my wages. Losing and being injured.
Favourite holiday resort: South of France.
Favourite TV star, male and female: Lenny Henry (left) and Maggie Thatcher.
Favourite activity on day off: Sometimes play golf.
Favourite singers: Stevie Wonder and Barbra Streisand.
After-match routine: I go out with my girlfriend and some of the other players.
Best friend: My grandad.
Biggest influence on career: My dad and Colin Harvey, the Everton reserve coach.
International honours: England Under21 cap.
Personal ambition: To win trophies with Everton and play for England.
If not a player what job would you do: psychiatrist.
Which person in the world would you most like to meet? Olivia Newton-John.

Full Name: Lee Carsley
Birthplace: Birmingham.
Birthdate: February 29, 1974.
Height: 5ft 10in.
Weight: 12st 6lb.
Previous clubs: Derby, Blackburn, Coventry.
Married: To Louisa.
Car: X5.
Favourite newspaper: Whatever's at the training ground.
Favourite player: Damien Duff's got real potential.
Promising team-mate: Wayne Rooney.

NOW: 2003

Favourite other team: I used to watch Villa, Blues, West Brom, Wolves and Walsall as a kid - and still look out for them all.
Football hero of childhood: Bryan Robson.
Favourite other sports: Sleeping!
Most difficult opponent: Dean Sturridge in training at Derby.
Most memorable match: Making my professional debut for Derby County at Swindon. We drew 1-1 but I stayed in the squad from that game.
Biggest disappointment: Relegations with Blackburn and Coventry.
Friendliest away fans: Haven't had too many problems.
Favourite food-drink: My wife's Sunday roast and mineral water - I'm teetotal.
Miscellaneous likes-dislikes: Spending time with my wife and three kids. Ignorant people or getting injured.
Favourite holiday resort: Spain.

Favourite TV star: I'm addicted to Big Brother, so whoever wins each series. Kylie - does that count?
Favourite activity on day off: Driving back to the Midlands to see the family.
Favourite singers: Linkin Park.
After-match routine: Home to see the kids. The days of going out are over for me.
Best friend: I have a few.
Biggest influence on my career: My family, Jim Smith, Steve McLaren and Arthur Cox at Derby.
International honours: full Republic of Ireland.
Personal ambition: To keep playing top-flight football for as long as possible.
If not a player, what job would you do: Help kids who are less fortunate in life.
Which person in the world would you most like to meet: Mart Poom. I cut up a new pair of his designer jeans at Derby and he never found out who did it. Now's the time to own up!

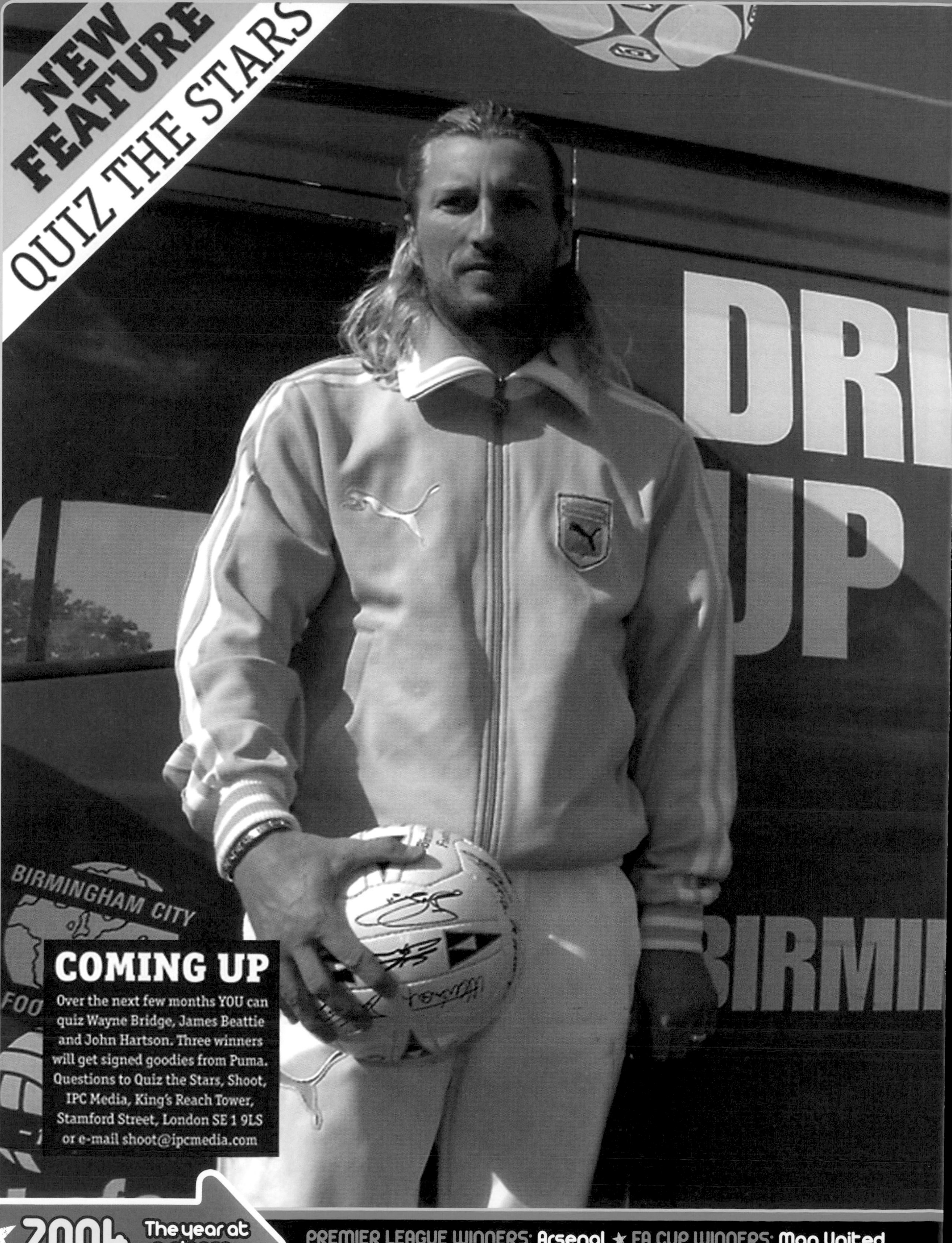

BIRMINGHAM CITY

FOO

COMING UP

Over the next few months YOU can quiz Wayne Bridge, James Beattie and John Hartson. Three winners will get signed goodies from Puma. Questions to Quiz the Stars, Shoot, IPC Media, King's Reach Tower, Stamford Street, London SE 1 9LS or e-mail shoot@ipcmedia.com

DRI
UP

BIRMI

TRUE BLUE

ROBBIE SAVAGE DOESN'T SHIRK A CHALLENGE, SO YOUR QUESTIONS ON BEING HATED, THAT DUMP IN THE REF'S LOO AND VIDEO EVIDENCE SHOULDN'T BE A PROBLEM…

BRAVING THE BRUMMIE: COLIN MITCHELL SAVAGE SNAPS: IAN CHAPMAN

ROBBIE SAVAGE IS HURT. It's not because of a crunching tackle from an opponent looking for revenge. It's not even the vicious taunts from fans who just love to hate him.

The controversial Birmingham midfielder is "gutted" by the FIFA ban that will see him miss Wales' forthcoming World Cup qualifying match against England following his sending off against Northern Ireland in September.

Amazingly, for such a competitive player, it was the first red card of his career. Bookings may have flown his way like confetti at a wedding, but this time it was different.

Robbie feels as though he has been dealt an injustice, not just by the sending off when he reacted to a wild lunge from Michael Hughes, but also the fact that he was denied a personal hearing and refused permission to go before a sporting arbitration panel.

"I'm really devastated," admits Robbie, who was set to take legal action to beat the ban, until he realised his cause was futile. There was also the chance of a legal bill which could have been in excess of £30,000.

"I'll be there, cheering the lads on against England but I am absolutely gutted not to be on the pitch. But what can I say? I am a big boy I have got to learn to take it on the chin, even though it was wrong," Robbie told **Shoot**.

"It would have been up there among the biggest games of my career and I have just got to look forward now to the England game at the Millennium Stadium. There are two games and if I did have to miss one… I would rather play at the Millennium."

After a tough workout at Birmingham City's training ground, Robbie launched into his next task of the day…. getting stuck into questions from **Shoot** readers…

WHAT CHANCE HAVE YOUR OLD CLUB LEICESTER OF BOUNCING STRAIGHT BACK UP TO THE PREMIERSHIP?
IAN WHALLEY ST. HELENS, MERSEYSIDE **WINNER**
"I think this year it's going to be really difficult for them to come back in the first year, like they did last time. That was fantastic. Obviously they have lost Muzzy Izzet to us, Les Ferdinand who scored a lot of goals, and they have lost Paul Dickov. But if

they do come back I will be delighted for them as Micky Adams is a fantastic boss. I like Leicester and I always look for their results."

EVER CONSIDERED PLAYING IN A MICHAEL "I'M A NICE GUY" OWEN MASK TO KEEP YOURSELF OUT OF STRIFE?
STEVE FAIRCLOUGH, CRAWLEY, SUSSEX.
"No, no… I don't like that one, it's a rubbish question, next one."

DO YOU ENJOY THE FACT THAT YOU ARE UNIVERSALLY HATED BY THE FANS OF OTHER CLUBS?
GUY THOMAS, EPSOM, SURREY.
"I don't enjoy it, but it does tell me I must be doing something right for the club I play for. That's not a mark of disrespect because I'm sure if I moved to their club they would cheer me. I think they would like me in their team. It applies to any player who does the business."

YOU ARE KNOWN AS AN AGGRESSIVE PLAYER. WERE YOU LIKE THAT WHEN YOU PLAYED IN JUNIOR FOOTBALL?
KRISTIAN JOHNSON, CREETING ST. MARY, IPSWICH. **WINNER**
"No I wasn't, I was a totally different player I actually had skill when I was younger (laughs) and I used to score a lot of goals. I was the top scorer in my local league, I think I scored 75 goals in one season, but I am a totally different player now. I was a striker then…"

DO YOU REGRET SH**TING IN REFEREE GRAHAM POLL'S CHANGING ROOM TOILET AT HALF-TIME DURING A MATCH – AND BEING FINED £10,000?
SIMON GODDARD, AYLESBURY, BUCKS.
"I don't regret it, I still honestly say I was not in the wrong. It is a well-known fact that there was no toilet available, the only one was the referee's. It is not about doing it in the referee's toilet, it is about going to the toilet full stop. I am a human being and human beings are meant to go to the toilet! I just went to the referee's and if I had to

make the decision again, I would probably do exactly the same."

WHAT IS THE BEST AND THE WORST SONG THAT YOU HAVE HEARD SUNG ABOUT YOU AND WHY?
STEVEN O'HARA, CHELMSLEY WOOD, BIRMINGHAM. **WINNER**
"The Blues have a song and it goes: 'We Love you Robbie, because you have got blonde hair; we love you because you are everywhere; we love you Robbie because you play for The Blues.' That's a good song! It's great to have a song about you and that one is a bit different to all the other boring ones, it's a good one. The worst… how many do you want? Every song is a bad one, other than that one."

WHAT IS THE BEST ONE LINER THAT YOU HAVE USED TO WIND UP AN OPPONENT? DID YOU GET A REACTION?
(ALSO STEVEN O'HARA).
"I think I said to Lothar Matthaus (former Germany skipper) the Hungary manager: 'Who are you?' when he ran on the pitch to confront me. That got a reaction, even though he has won the

Lothar who?

World Cup 25 times!" (Laughs out loud).

DO YOU REGRET THAT YOU DIDN'T GET A CONTRACT AT MAN UNITED FOLLOWING THE SUCCESS OF THE YOUTH TEAM?
CHRIS MCNICHOLAS, LONDON.

"Yes, I do. I would loved to have stayed there, and throughout my career, but obviously it

Robbie's marching orders against Northern Ireland.

didn't happen. I still wouldn't have changed the way it has gone for me since. I have thoroughly enjoyed my life since I left, I've had my own successes and wouldn't change it for the world. I take my hat off to the lads who have stayed." (Gary Neville, Nicky Butt and David Beckham were part of the same FA Youth Cup-winning side as Robbie).

IN THE LIGHT OF SOME OF THE DECISIONS IN THE WALES v NORTHERN IRELAND GAME, DO YOU THINK IT'S NOW THE TIME FOR FOOTBALL TO MAKE MORE USE OF TECHNOLOGY?
ROGER WHITE, SURREY.

"The thing with my sending off is that FIFA don't let you appeal. They watch the video but then they still gave me a ban. Everyone knows it wasn't a sending off, but they still ban you for one game and you have no right of appeal, which I think is strange. That said I wouldn't like to see much video stuff in football because it would stop the flow of the game, it is great just as it is.

"Some of the rules should definitely be changed though. For example the yellow cards for a shirt over your head when you celebrate a goal. The people who make these rules have probably never played the game, it is shocking really.

"Sin bin? No way, keep it how it is."

WHAT MUSIC DO YOU LIKE TO LISTEN TO IN YOUR SPARE TIME?
TOM FLYNN, HOLYWOOD, BIRMINGHAM. (HE'S ACTUALLY AT THE TRAINING GROUND, WAITING TO GRAB ROBBIE'S AUTOGRAPH, RIGHT).

"He's come a long way! (Robbie laughs, as if his fan has arrived from LA). I don't really listen to that much music, but if I am in my house I like Lionel Richie, The Greatest Hits."

HOME IS WHERE THE HEART IS...

THE SNARLING, SNAPPING Robbie Savage you see on the pitch is a different person off it.

Fans queue up outside of Birmingham's training ground to grab his autograph, club officials chat and joke with him and team-mates can only laugh as they are the brunt of his pranks and wind-ups.

Former Chelsea star Jesper Gronkjaer got some heavy stick when his top-of-the-range car wouldn't start. Robbie challenged him to get a better motor, then moved swiftly across the training ground car park to see if he could help out.

With one turn of the ignition key his team-mate was mobile.

"He's from Denmark, you know," laughed Robbie taunting winger Gronkjaer who departed with a wave and a smile.

Robbie's happy-go-lucky manner is testament to how much he is enjoying life at Birmingham. His move from Leicester in May 2002 for £2.5m has proved a great bit of business.

"It's been fantastic, probably the best two and a half years of my life really," admits the Wrexham-born player. "I have really taken the club to heart and am really enjoying playing under the manager.

"Obviously, now we have got in some better players it is the best

Hang on, there's a stain on that shirt.

The man they just love to hate.

squad since I have been here and it is all looking good for the future," said the man whose own career looked to be away from St. Andrews last summer.

Robbie, 30 this month, admitted: "Everton have probably made about four or five bids in total but the manager doesn't want to let me go.

"From my point of view, I am happy and delighted to still be here. It's nice to know that the manager still wants me, he could

Robbie meets the man from Holywood.

have sold me but he sees me as a big part of his plans.

"When you get linked with other clubs some people ask if it is nice, others ask if it is distracting. All I can say is that you have to keep on playing well, and if other teams keep on wanting you, you must be doing something right for your own club."

Again, all that could have changed at the start of the season with Brum's Geordie boss Steve Bruce linked with a move to St. James' Park.

"Newcastle was a huge job for him but obviously he didn't go and that was a huge boost for all of the players," said Robbie.

"The vast majority of the lads - including me - signed because of the manager, so if he had gone it would have been a massive, massive blow to the football club.

"It could have upset the balance, just when things are going so smoothly."

Smooth isn't however the word you would use to describe Birmingham's under-performing start to the

season. The arrival of Gronkjaer and Mario Melchiot from Chelsea; record signing Emile Heskey from Liverpool and Leicester's Muzzy Izzet should have kick-started City's new term. Instead, it's been a bit of a rocky road.

"The squad we have got now is better than we had last year and the start to the season is not as good as we would have liked," admitted Robbie.

"Saying that we could have taken something out of every game. Portsmouth away we drew (1-1) but should have won and Chelsea home we should have won (lost 0-1).

"Tottenham were the better team (lost 1-0) and Middlesbrough was probably the only game we shouldn't have taken something out of (lost 2-1).

"It's not been the best start and it can only get better. We have got to gel but we don't want to still be saying that after ten games.

"We have to gel as soon as we can to get the points on the board because it is a tough old season."

Brucey wonders if Robbie has been to his loo.

...7...8...9...10...

IMPROVE YOUR SKILLS

TAKE THE FROSTIES FOOTBALL CHALLENGE

THE MYTHICAL WORLD OF MADRID

The fanatical "theatre-loving" Madrid fans.

COOL AND SUPER-CONFIDENT... but it was a different Michael Owen who arrived at the Bernabeu to start work for the first time.

"I walked into the changing room for my first training session and was really nervous I just didn't want them to think they had bought a dud," laughed Michael.

"It is the same for anyone moving to a new club, school or job. You are always a bit wary and hope you make a good impression. I was no different and after the first couple of training sessions I was okay.

"But walking in there and seeing all these big stars around does put a bit of pressure on. Thankfully that stage is out of the way now.

"I never knew what to expect and when you come back to England everyone asks 'what is it like there?' It really is like a mythical club, everyone is interested in what happens.

"The players are some of the best in the world but I found the team spirit is good despite having so many brilliant stars. Everyone mixes in and has a laugh. It's a good changing room to be in."

However, playing in Spain is a totall[y] new ball game for Michael, not least b[...] he's experiencing many of the stadia [...] the first time.

"It is a strange atmosphere, the gro[...] especially. In Spain the grounds are ve[...] compared to the English games. If you[...] went to the game you would probably [...] it is not that fanatical but it is more t[...] where people come to be entertained[...]

"But when you go around the count[...] your bus pulls up or you are driving o[...] the stadium after the game in your ca[...] absolutely fanatical. Twice as big as a[...]

"I live just outside the town, but w[...] you go into town you get recognised, [...] odd photograph, but not too much. I'[...] been accepted – the banners and the [...] with my name.

"The first time I heard them singin[...] name I was filled with a lot of pride. [...] always nice to earn the respect of you[...] mates, but to earn the respect of the [...] as well is not easy in a place like Mad[...]

MICHAEL IS DETERMINED to add his name to the short list of English players who[...] established themselves overseas. In fact he is convinced the move will help him tak[...] already successful career on to another level.

"I am sure it can't do me any harm!" he said. "I am playing with top players, it is a[...] fantastic, high quality league and I am in one of the top teams in the world."

It also helps if you have friends in the dressing room and one of Michael's other f[...] sports, golf, ensures he has an active social life. "We have a little golf school. Ronal[...] and the second keeper, Cesar Sanchez, play along with Guti. We go after training ev[...] other week or when we can. My handicap is eight at the moment – I was seven last y[...] I went up a stroke so I can get an extra shot and try to win!" smiled Michael.

So what does he miss most about England? Fish and chips, HP sauce, Coronation [...]

"My house" he says without hesitation. "To be fair, the food out in Spain is one of [...] positives. But it (the country home near Northop) is my dream house. It has my two [...] my horse and all the land that I want. I got it perfect for living in and then I had to [...]

Michael does admit that watching his other favourite sport, horse racing, on TV i[...] best." But he's already booked a box for his family at the Epsom Derby and for Asco[...] are two trips to look forward to when we get back in the s[...] Not wishing my life away though!"

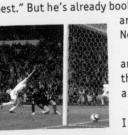

Meanwhile, girlfriend Louise Bonsall has joined a local [...] and daughter Gemma is in a new nursery. "She spends thr[...] there every day and is making her own friends. She is talk[...] a bit now with a few 'holas' and 'gracias'.

"We have made friends and we go out to restaurants. I'[...] I made the right decision."

REIGNING IN SPAIN

COMING HOME, HE'S COMING HOME... OR IS HE? **SHOOT** TALKS TO **MICHAEL OWEN** ABOUT HIS FOOTBALLING FUTURE. **WORDS: Colin Mitchell**

Michael notches up another goal at the Bernabeu.

MICHAEL OWEN WANTS it to be known he loves life in Spain. He thinks it's great to be part of the mighty Real Madrid squad. And he has no plans to return to England.

Linked in recent months with a quick trip back to the Premiership, the former Liverpool striker's main concern is keeping a place in the Spanish side's starting line-up. But he's confident he can be a success at the Bernabeu.

"From the position I was in at the start with Raul, Morientes and Ronaldo, a lot of people told me I was crazy to come here," Michael told **Shoot** in an exclusive interview.

"But how many times will you be asked to play for Real Madrid? I might have been all those things people said, but I knew that you can't keep a good man down for too long.

"One month I am on top of the world, then for the next month I am sitting on the bench. I went through

> **"PEOPLE SAID I WAS CRAZY. BUT HOW MANY TIMES ARE YOU ASKED TO PLAY FOR MADRID?"**

a patch of starting eight or nine games on the spin and being a regular and they dropped Raul back into midfield so that was a nice feather in the cap.

"Since Christmas I have been back on the bench a bit but at least the fans and the management now know what I can do. I have scored a lot of goals and that is a pleasing thing. It's not job accomplished, but so far I am happy considering where I started."

Michael, who has seen Fernando Morientes leave his new club to join Liverpool, added: "I am only 25 and hopefully have a good, long career ahead of me. There are plenty of things that are in the future for me. I don't know 'when' or 'if' and I wouldn't say 'yes' or 'no' to anything.

"But I am really enjoying it in Spain. Yes, I do miss certain things about not being in England, but I also feel I've improved on a lot of things being here.

"It is well documented I don't like sitting on ▶

A FAMILY A[...]

THE CLOSENESS OF the O[...]
legendary – with Michael [...]
de sac so they could live in [...]

So his move abroad prob[...]
of a shock to them than th[...]
when his £8m deal , which [...]
Nunez move the other way [...]

"If there is one thing th[...]
home comforts, being arou[...]
friends, being in your hou[...]
had bought an old country [...]

"I had just had my hous[...]
virtually the minute it wa[...]
leaving. They are the thin[...]
will always be there. My w[...]
once a month and my mun[...]
every weekend so we have[...]

Michael also has his En[...]
Beckham and defender Jo[...]
company, which has help[...]

"It is always nice to g[...]
your own language, talk [...]
and whatever game you h[...]
previous night."

Don't expect him to g[...]
though. Michael aims to [...]
Spanish, I have a lesson [...]
is difficult as we often h[...]

"I have the language [...]
listen to it on the way in [...]
I would have to learn a f[...]
when I first started play[...]
never thought I would p[...]

"Real was something [...]
maybe once a year when [...]
Now I am living in a diff[...]

the bench so let's hope things improve and I don't have to sit there too much! That obviously wouldn't do me any good.

"Would I return to Liverpool? I'm very happy at Madrid but I would have nothing against it. I left Liverpool on good terms and they are still the first result I look out for. I have a lot of friends there. I have no bitterness at all to Liverpool and they are still very close to my heart."

With speculation rife that he could return to the Premier League with Arsenal, Chelsea or Liverpool and Newcastle boss Graeme Souness publicly admitting an interest in the England hit-man, Michael is flattered.

But he now feels he has made his mark in La Liga, and not just because of his great goal tally, despite limited starts.

"I think if you ask anyone's opinion of me in Spain they will all rate me as a player and the fans sing my name. They have taken to me, which is a great thing and I think I have gained the respect of the other players, which is also important," said Michael.

But his new life didn't get off to such a good start when he arrived with girlfriend Louise and daughter Gemma.

"It was tough to begin with, we lived in a hotel for four months with a one-year-old daughter. We were trying to make friends in a foreign country, but the baby needed to be in bed by 8pm and there was no one to look after her.

"We had to switch the lights off and literally sit in the dark for three hours until we went to bed. It was difficult to settle in but the last few months we have been in the house and settled.

"My football also seemed to pick up when I was happy off the pitch and now I am making more and more friends, and I don't just mean when I am playing."

A NEW CH[...]

In goalscoring form for Madrid against Real Betis.

WAYNE'S WORLD

WITH A YEAR AT OLD TRAFFORD UNDER HIS BELT, **SHOOT** GETS A GLIMPSE OF WHAT REALLY MAKES **WAYNE ROONEY** TICK.
WORDS: Frank Tennyson

H E'S THE MOST famous 20-year-old on the planet. A star striker with the expectations of both club and country on his broad shoulders, yet he still plays with the exuberance and flair of a youngster having a kick-about in the park!

Signed by Man United in the summer of 2004 (for a fee which should eventually reach £30m,) the former Everton man marked his debut with a scintillating hat-trick in a Champions League tie with Fenerbahce.

A month later he scored the second goal which ended Arsenal's 49-game unbeaten run before his consistently brilliant form propelled The Red Devils to the FA Cup Final. Only a ultra-tense penalty shoot-out denied Wayne a winner's medal in his first season at Old Trafford.

This season he has maintained the kind of form that prompted Sir Alex Ferguson to label him "the best young player this country has seen in the past 30 years.".

In his new DVD *Wayne Rooney – My First Year at Manchester United,* the England superstar reflects on a year that he will never forget…

CAN YOU REMEMBER BACK TO WHEN YOU HEARD MAN UNITED WERE TRYING TO SIGN YOU?
"Obviously I was delighted that a club of Manchester United's size was interested in me. I told my advisors and my agent that I wanted to go there and to make sure that it

HE'S ONE IN A MILLION

What they had to say about the Roonster...

RYAN GIGGS
"Great players do things instinctively and Wayne definitely tries things other players don't. You want exciting players and Wayne is certainly one of those, a young player who is just going to get better and better. There was great excitement throughout the club – and for me personally – to have such a talent, and to play with such a talent."

RUUD VAN NISTELROOY
"I saw him train and saw that he was naturally ready to deal with the expectations, even for someone so young. He is mentally really strong."

RIO FERDINAND
"He goes out like he is playing for his Sunday League team when he was a kid – it's just that he's in a United kit and playing in front of 67,000 fans."

SIR ALEX FERGUSON
"He's a product of being brought up just thinking about football. There are many examples of that – Roy Keane, Bryan Robson, Mark Hughes – who combine that great energy and passion to play football all the time. It doesn't matter the kind of game, you get the same desire and commitment every time. It's refreshing to see someone so young have that."

PAUL SCHOLES
"He's got everything, the way he takes players on, the way he scores goals. When you have someone like that in your side, you are confident that you can win any game."

ROY KEANE
"He never seems to feel the pressure of the big games. His abilities are there for everyone to see. He's an outstanding young player and hopefully he will improve even more. "

WES BROWN
"Wayne came in to the club and made an impact straight away. Because he's such a talent, he's already won a few awards and I'm sure there are more to come."

---

happened. Then it was down to the two clubs to agree a price. I wanted it all out of the way but the talks got really close, then stalled a few times – and it was right up to the transfer deadline before it happened. It was a bit anxious for a while but we got there in the end.

"When I signed there were loads of fans waiting outside for me which was brilliant. The next day I was having my first Manchester United training session."

WHAT WAS IT LIKE ON YOUR FIRST DAY AT TRAINING?
"I was really nervous. You see the likes of Keano and Giggsy sitting there looking at you! It was weird but the lads were brilliant. I went and shook everyone's hands and I settled in really quickly."

AS A YOUNG EVERTONIAN WHICH UNITED PLAYERS DID YOU FEAR MOST?
"Probably Cantona and Solskjaer in particular – he always seemed to score against us! Becks and Scholesy used to play well too and then there is Mark Hughes, who was also at Everton for a while. It's great to think that I am playing for the same club as those great players."

IF YOU HAD TO PICK ONE?
"Probably Ollie (Solskjaer). When he came to Goodison he stood out. He worked hard, and always scored great goals against Everton. I always hated to see him play against us!"

TELL US ABOUT YOUR FIRST UNITED GAME – A HAT-TRICK IN THE CHAMPIONS LEAGUE AGAINST FENERBAHCE!
"The manager told me a couple of days before that I was going to play and obviously I was delighted. It was my debut and the fans were brilliant. I relished it, really. It took me 10-15 minutes to get into the game and after I settled down everything obviously went really well. It was hard physically because I hadn't played for a while. I nearly dropped dead at the end!"

THAT MEANT THE FANS IMMEDIATELY TOOK YOU TO THEIR HEARTS...
"I think it's brilliant. From the first game I played, they all sang my name. I just want to give my best for the team and win the game for the club. I think the fans see that. Hearing them sing my name gives me a real boost but

at the same time you have to try and blank it out a bit, not get too carried away and focus on the game. Although, the atmosphere at Old Trafford can be frightening…"

WHAT EFFECT HAS FERGIE HAD ON YOU CAREER?

"He's made me aware of what he wants and expects from me and the team. He's a brilliant manager and everyone around the place has the most respect for him. If you look at what he has achieved in the game, there is no-one better, in my view. If you ask any player who has signed for the club, he's brilliant. He gives us his mobile number so if we ever need something he's there for us."

"When I first met him I was a bit nervous, if I'm honest. The only time I had seen him

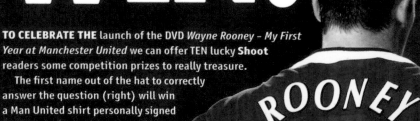

was on the touchline and on the TV so to actually meet him was brilliant."

WHO ARE YOUR MATES IN THE UNITED DRESSING ROOM?

"Well, me Sheasy (John O'Shea), Rio (Ferdinand) and Wes (Brown) play computer games together at each other's houses. We're big fans of FIFA 2006. I always play with United and Ruud (Van Nistelrooy) is the top scorer, not me!"

WHO IS THE BEST TRAINER AT THE CLUB?

"Probably Scholesy. His ability, his passing, his shooting is brilliant – a great example for all the youngsters coming through. The worst? Wes – no I'm kidding, really. He's good too, it's just that we always try and take the mickey out of each other…"

HOW DO YOU LOOK BACK ON YOUR FIRST YEAR AT UNITED?

"It's everything I could have dreamed of, although without the trophies. I couldn't be happier, I've settled in brilliantly and I'm sure it will come. The expectation at this club is massive and you have to live up to that. You look round and see the trophies that United has won and it inspires you."

SPEAKING OF MISSING OUT ON TROPHIES, WHAT ARE YOUR MEMORIES OF THE FA CUP FINAL?

"We performed really well, played some nice football but unfortunately didn't take our chances. We lost on

penalties which we were really disappointed about. But we were more disappointed about the game – if we had taken our chances we would've won the cup."

ARE YOU CONFIDENT THAT YOU CAN GET YOURSELF A WINNER'S MEDAL COME MAY?

"For sure. Hopefully Chelsea will lose a few points and we can catch them up. They've had a good start but if they drop points, there is one team to catch them up – and that's us"

IS THE CHAMPIONS LEAGUE STILL THE HOLY GRAIL FOR UNITED?

"At this club we want to win every tournament we are in. First of all we want the league but of course the Champions League is massive for us too. The number of trophies won here in the past is frightening – the current set of lads want to add to that great history."

FINALLY, WHAT ARE YOUR AMBITIONS IN A MAN UNITED SHIRT?

"It's simple. A club this size should be winning trophies and I think we have a good enough squad to be doing exactly that."

JOE COLE

JOECOLE.COM

In his last column before the World Cup, Joe Cole hopes that England can live up to our expectations...

HERE WE GO, HERE WE GO...

 EVERYONE HAS BEEN talking about Theo Walcott. I had that kind of pressure when I was a young lad at West Ham and know it's important everyone leaves him alone, although I know it's not going to happen. I am sure he has good people around him and he will handle it.

Arsene Wenger's a top manager, Theo's at a great club and he has his family to rely on. The boy is going to be a great player, be it in this World Cup, the next one or even the one after that.

He has so much talent and he needs to ignore all the hype. We're lucky to have him here but he just has to get on playing his football and learning – and that's probably what he's happiest doing at the moment.

The injury to Wayne Rooney has been a massive blow, but there is still enough in the rest of the team. He is a loss but you change the system, you tweak things slowly and we can still go and beat teams. If this team comes together we have so many big name players... Owen, Beckham... and just look at the midfield. Steven Gerrard demonstrated in the FA Cup Final that he is one of the best of his type in the world and Frank Lampard is up there with him.

From a personal point of view, I go into this World Cup thinking there is not a lot that is going to surprise me on the pitch. I'm still young but very experienced and really, really looking forward to the finals.

For me, I just want to come in there, work hard and play in a winning side. I don't think you can ever dream how big it would be if we were to win the World Cup. It would just be incredible. I watched the rugby champions and the Ashes winners and all credit to their great achievements, but if England were to win the World Cup it would just be sensational. You wouldn't believe the size of it.

Hopefully the next time I write this column we'll be World Cup holders. Wish us well won't you...?

> "HOPEFULLY NEXT TIME I WRITE THIS COLUMN WE'LL BE WORLD CUP HOLDERS. WISH US WELL WON'T YOU...?"

WHERE WILL I PLAY?

IF I HAD A free choice in the England team then I would pick the centre of midfield but I've learned to enjoy the other positions as well.

For Chelsea I've played a lot of games on the right and for England, it's been mostly on the left. I'm happy to play anywhere though, just as long as I'm in the team.

I've been involved in two big tournaments now, the 2002 World Cup and Euro 2004 and in total I've played ten minutes of football, as a substitute against Sweden in Japan.

It was a great experience both times and invaluable to me but I have to admit I felt like a spare part at times, particularly in Portugal. It's marvellous to be in any England squad but at the end of the day I want to play.

I can look back now and take plenty from both experiences. I definitely feel more confident now, more established. I've just come off a good season at Chelsea and I'm ready for this.

We all are... obviously there is a doubt about Wayne Rooney and he would be a massive miss of he didn't make it but everyone is hoping he will be okay in time.

If not though, I still feel that we have the players and spirit in this squad to have a really successful World Cup.

LAST WORD

DAVID WEIR

» WHEN WAS THE LAST TIME YOU...

BOUGHT A NEW CD?
"That was when I got a present for my wife the other day. I think it was Mel C's album but I'm not too sure! She told me what album she wanted and I went to the shop and repeated it! Simple, eh?"

PAID TO WATCH A GAME?
"Blimey, that must have been a few years ago. I reckon it was when I was still at school and used to go to watch my local team Falkirk. These days, when I go home, I'll watch my former team Hearts. But I have to admit, I tend to tap someone up for a ticket. One of the perks of being a footballer, I guess."

SPLASHED OUT ON SOME DESIGNER GEAR?
"I'm really into clothes and I'm forever on the look-out for some new gear. Luckily, an old friend of mine owns a very nice shop in Falkirk called Exit, which has a great selection of designer labels. And being a mate, he takes care of me and gives me a good discount!"

WENT ON HOLIDAY?
"I got married last year and for the honeymoon we went to New York and Boston. Neither myself or my wife are the go-and-lay-on-the-beach-type so we went to see the sights and do a bit of shopping. And of course this meant hitting the shops in The Big Apple and spending a lot of money!"

WERE STUNNED BY A REFEREEING DECISION DURING A MATCH?
"I've got to be careful here as I don't want to get myself into trouble. But in the final minute of the Merseyside derby last month, Don Hutchison had a goal disallowed for some strange reason."

HAD A RUN-IN WITH SOMEONE AT THE CLUB?
"You'll always have a few throughout the season. Whenever you are beaten in a game and feelings are running high, there are going to be a few words said. The last rollicking I had was at Newcastle when one of their goals was down to me."

WERE THE VICTIM OF A PRACTICAL JOKE?
"Only the other week, actually. I bought a pair of new shoes and found them floating about in the bath when I came into the dressing rooms after training! This is one of David Unsworth's favourite tricks but he's still denying it. I'll get him back though, there's no worry on that score."

TREATED YOURSELF TO A BRAND NEW SET OF WHEELS?
"I bought a new car in September from a friend in Liverpool who works in an Audi garage. And, yep, of course he got me a decent deal!"

PLAYED IN A BRILLIANT ATMOSPHERE?
"That would have to be the Merseyside derby last month. The Scousers love their football and although it's a friendly kind of atmosphere, it still sends a few tingles down the back of your spine."

PLAYER FILE
Your guide to the stars and their lifestyles...

THIS MONTH: **ANDY JOHNSON**, CRYSTAL PALACE

NAME: Andrew James Johnson.
NICKNAME: AJ.
POSITION: Striker.
PREVIOUS CLUBS: Birmingham.
BIRTHPLACE: February 10, 1981, Bedford, England.
MARRIED: No.
CAR: Just got a new one – BMW X5.
MOBILE PHONE: Nokia.

FOOTBALL

BEST MOMENT IN FOOTBALL?
"Coming on for England to make my debut against Holland."

WORST MOMENT IN FOOTBALL?
"When I missed the deciding penalty for Birmingham to lose the League Cup Final against Liverpool (2001)."

HAS THE BOSS EVER GIVEN YOU A TICKING OFF?
"Not as yet - I'm a good lad."

THE BEST PLAYER YOU HAVE EVER FACED?
"Thierry Henry."

YOU'VE JUST BEEN GIVEN PERMISSION TO SIGN ANY ONE PLAYER YOU WANT FOR YOUR TEAM – WHO WOULD YOU BUY?
"Ronaldinho. He's the best player in the world."

TELL US SOMETHING FUNNY ABOUT ONE OF YOUR TEAM-MATES.
"Danny Butterfield has the worst haircut in football. He's grown it long to cover his ears because they're so big."

WHAT'S THE BIGGEST WIND-UP YOU'VE BEEN THE VICTIM OF?
"Having my clothes cut up by Danny Butterfield and Shaun Derry."

ANY SUPERSTITIONS?
"Loads. One of mine is if I wear a suit and have a good game then I wear it again the next match."

LIFESTYLE

MOST FAMOUS PERSON YOU'VE MET?
"David Beckham."

EastEnders' Michelle Ryan plays two up front.

FAVOURITE TV PROGRAMME?
"EastEnders."

WHO IS IN CHARGE OF THE CLUB STEREO AND WHAT DOES HE PLAY?
"We all choose a song to go on one CD. So if it's a 16-man squad we have 16 different songs, that way no-one can have a moan."

THE LAST CD YOU BOUGHT?
"Usher (right)."

DILEMMA QUESTIONS

SOMEONE IN THE CROWD THROWS A £1 COIN AT YOU. DO YOU PICK IT UP AND STICK IT IN YOUR SOCK? GO RUNNING TO THE REFEREE? OR JUMP IN THE CROWD?
"I'd pick it up. Footballers don't get paid that much!"

A FAN ASKS FOR YOUR AUTOGRAPH BUT THINKS YOU ARE SOMEBODY ELSE. DO YOU TELL THEM TO CLEAR OFF OR JUST SIGN IT ANYWAY?
"I'd just sign it anyway."

WHAT MUSIC IS IN YOUR CAR AT THE MOMENT?
"R and B. Usher is my favorite."

FAVOURITE DESIGNER?
"Prada."

WORST DRESSED TEAM-MATE?
"Aki Riihilahti. He is just poor. He can't even do his shoes up."

LAST BOOK YOU READ?
"George Best."

IF NOT A FOOTBALLER WHAT WOULD YOU BE?
"I'd probably have been a roofer or something like that."

IF MONEY WAS NO OBJECT, WHAT CAR WOULD YOU BUY?
"The same one I have now."

TAKE YOUR PICK...

GABY LOGAN OR HELEN CHAMBERLAIN
"Gaby Logan."

TRAINING OR SLEEP-IN?
"Sleep-in."

DEL BOY OR BO SELECTA?
"Del Boy."

TERRESTRIAL OR SKY SPORTS?
"Sky Sports."

HEAVY METAL OR POP?
"Pop."

IPOD OR WALKMAN?
"Ipod."

CURRY OR STEAK?
"Steak."

SUNDERLAND

PLAYER FACTFILE
GORDON

Full name: Craig Sinclair Gordon.

Born: Edinburgh, December 31, 1982.

Position: Goalkeeper.

Height: 6ft 4in.

Weight: 13st 1lb.

Did you know? Craig made his Hearts debut in 2002 at the age of 19, and has since been the Bank of Scotland Premier League Young Player of the Season and the Scottish Football Writers' Association Player of the Year.

KEANE TO JOIN!

CRAIG GORDON ADMITS THAT ROY KEANE TALKED HIM INTO A £9m RECORD-BREAKING MOVE TO SUNDERLAND...

CRAIG GORDON'S FUTURE as a Hearts player had been on the line for months before Sunderland won the race for the Scotland keeper's signature.

A whole host of Premiership sides had been linked with the lanky shot-stopper, including Arsenal, Fulham and Aston Villa before he agreed a five-year contract at The Stadium of Light.

The blarney of Black Cats boss Roy Keane beat off a serious attempt by Villa to sign the Hearts skipper and prise him away from the club he'd supported since he was a boy.

The Wearsiders have paid a club record £7m up front for their new man between the sticks with a further £2m possible, depending on appearances and progress – and that could lead to a new British record fee for a keeper.

Craig had been involved at Tynecastle as a player from the age of 12, eventually taking over the captain's armband from Steven Pressley last December. But as unrest grew over the arrival of many overseas players and the revolving door policy involving managers, it looked odds-on that Craig would eventually have to move.

Having established himself at Scotland's No.1 keeper he also had big ambitions to prove himself in the English top-flight. **Shoot** caught up with the shot-stopper to get his views on club and country...

QUITE A FEW CLUBS WERE CHASING YOU, SO WHY SUNDERLAND?

"As soon as I spoke to Roy [Keane] there was only one place I was going to go. He doesn't settle for second best and that is a great trait to have in your personality.

"I've never made a secret of the fact I want to play in the Premiership, it's one of the top leagues in the world and it will be good to test myself there. It's a massive place to be."

YOUR TRANSFER DRAGGED ON FOR QUITE A WHILE...

"I was aware of the interest five or six weeks before and it was a long time coming. Sunderland were very patient to see this transfer through and I am grateful for that. The facilities here are excellent and Roy is a good young manager.

> "AS SOON AS I SPOKE TO ROY THERE WAS ONLY ONE PLACE I WAS GOING TO GO. HE DOESN'T SETTLE FOR SECOND BEST AND THAT IS A GREAT TRAIT TO HAVE IN YOUR PERSONALITY."

He told me about his ambitions for Sunderland and the future he sees for the club and what he had to say was great."

HOW DO YOU THINK YOU WILL GET ON HERE?

"I think you have to go into a season being as positive as you can and I don't think anyone would be happy just with survival. We are here to be as successful as possible in this league.

"I am sure that there will be a lot more stability down here than at Hearts. They do like to change a manager up there! It isn't easy but you have to deal with it."

SO WAS IT DIFFICULT IN THE END TO LEAVE TYNECASTLE?

"I've supported Hearts since I was a young lad and my hero was the keeper Gilles Rousset. He was still at the club when I signed in 1999 and I managed to train for half a season with him before he retired. To be able to do that was fantastic for me.

"I could not turn down a chance to play in the English Premier League. It is a massive opportunity. Sunderland is an ambitious club with a fanatical support and I think that is something similar to Hearts. The fans are fanatical about their club.

"Hearts will always be my team so it is important to go to a city where football is a way of life. I will go back to support the boys when I can. It was a joy to play for Hearts because I am a fan."

SCOTTISH KEEPERS COME IN FOR STICK SOUTH OF THE BORDER...

"I think the fans have this stereotype that I would love to prove wrong with my performances here over the next few years."

WHAT HIS NEW BOSS SAYS...

Roy Keane's view on his new £9m acquisition...
"Craig will be a good signing for us. He is a good age and has good experience. I just hope we can take him onto the next level because there is room for improvement with every player.

"He is a very talented player. We do not get bogged down by transfer records or whatever because they are there to be broken and they will continue to rise. It shouldn't worry players and they have just got to concentrate on their game.

"The way fees are going up is only going to get a lot worse. But it is like everything else; if you want quality in life, if it's a nice car or a nice house, you have to pay for it."

THERE'S ALSO CRITICISM THAT THERE ARE ONLY TWO TEAMS IN THE SPL, RANGERS AND CELTIC!

"Last season no, there wasn't just two teams. The previous term Hearts came close and they certainly have the capabilities to challenge. If they have quality international players then maybe they could challenge again. But I agree, Rangers and Celtic are quite a way ahead of the rest. You only have to look at the league table."

WHEN YOU PLAY TEAMS OTHER THAN THE OLD FIRM IS THAT A LESSER GAME?

"I don't think so. When you are in the Scottish Premier League you know everyone who is in it and you play each other three or four times a season, depending on which half of the league you finish in.

"You know these grounds inside out and you have probably been there every year you have played as there's only one relegation spot. That can cause a problem because most players realise what they are going to get and complacency can creep in."

WHAT DOES IT MEAN TO YOU TO PLAY FOR SCOTLAND?

"It means an awful lot. The Tartan Army are absolutely fantastic and to play in front of those guys is incredible. They don't stop singing for 90 minutes and have an absolute ball wherever they go. They have a party but still concentrate on the football.

"It's also great to travel around Europe and play against top quality opposition. We've had a great start to our [Euro 2008] campaign this year so we still have that great hope we can make a major finals in the next few years."

ARE YOU NERVOUS WHEN YOU TAKE TO THE PITCH FOR YOUR COUNTRY?

"Of course the heart misses a beat a little. You are standing there singing the national anthem and they are all singing with you. In front of 50,000 at Hampden you get a great atmosphere or if you go away from home you can have 6,000 with you, which is an incredible figure.

"That's more than you can get at an SPL game – you can have 3,000 or 4,000, depending on where it is, so to go elsewhere in Europe and the back of beyond and take such support with you brings it home how much football means to people in Scotland. It'd be an honour to bring them success."

THERE APPEARS TO BE A NEW DAWN FOR

FACT
If Sunderland have to fork out the full £9m fee for Craig, it would make him the world's third most expensive keeper behind Gianluigi Buffon of Juventus (£32.6m) and Inter Milan's Angelo Peruzzi (£10.5m).

SCOTLAND AT THE MOMENT...

"I think more players are coming through. The SPL is having to bring through younger players because of financial restraints, they can no longer afford to bring foreign stars in and that can only be good for the Scottish youngsters hoping to play at a high level.

"We've also got a few people in England now, the likes of James McFadden at Everton and Darren Fletcher at Man United, so when we get them together with the young lads for squads, a lot of experience is passed around."

HAS THE NUMBER OF FOREIGNERS IN SCOTLAND AFFECTED THE GAME THERE?

"Possibly, although I now think it is starting to go back the other way with both Rangers and Celtic signing more Scottish players. I think we have now gone through that phase, that young players are now coming through, and hopefully we can see that continue."

AND WHAT ABOUT YOUR OWN CAREER?

"I'm 25 this year and I think you just have to keep progressing no matter how old you are. Whether you are 25 or 35 you must work hard and try to improve your game. I have been playing in the first-team since I was 20 so I have gained quite a bit of experience."

Niall Quinn wishes he could sign some of the Creating Chances side...

CREATING CHANCES

Big supporter: Ledley King

PREMIER LEAGUE UNVEILS FANTASTIC NEW COMMUNITY INITIATIVE

THE PREMIER LEAGUE has launched a brand new community initiative, "Creating Chances", to showcase the huge amount of good work that top-flight football clubs do in their local communities and for good causes and charities.

At a star-studded launch in London last month, 20 players from across the League came together to highlight this work, and show precisely how the Premier League and their clubs are more committed to the "other side" of the game than ever.

The Premier League and its 20 clubs will invest an estimated £122m this season in community projects, charities and other good causes, representing an increase of more than 50 per cent since 2003.

Tottenham captain Ledley King, one of the players at the launch, is a huge fan of the scheme. He said: "It's lovely for the lads to be able to support this great cause. When I was a kid of ten or 12, if I'd had the opportunity to get involved in something like this, I would have remembered it for a long, long time.

"When I was that age, I don't think I'd ever seen or met a footballer, so for us to turn up on their doorsteps and show our support is great. It's fantastic if we can give the kids some help to achieve what they want to achieve."

There are three key elements to the Creating Chances initiative...

1 Places for Players will involve 200 Premier League players supporting a number of charities and good causes in September, raising awareness of and funds for the work that those organisations do. More than 400 good causes will benefit, either by players getting involved in their work or from a £2,000 cash donation direct from the Premier League.

2 Your Shot is a scheme that will see each Barclays Premier League club offer one of their most deserving fans the opportunity to win a once-in-a-lifetime match day experience.

3 Premier League All Stars is a seven-a-side knockout competition that will be played during the Creating Chances week of action in September when 60 fans win the opportunity to play with top-flight legends and celebrities in teams representing all 20 Barclays Premier

League clubs. Star names like Fabrizio Ravanelli, Paul Merson, Ray Wilkins and Ruud Gullit are back in training and more big names from the worlds of football and showbiz will join them. The teams will play in official club kits and compete for a £300,000 prize fund which will be donated to charities of the clubs' choice.

THE BOSS SAYS...

Richard Scudamore, chief executive of the Premier League
"Community engagement is now woven into the fabric of football and the size and scope of that commitment today really is something of which the Premier League, our clubs and the players can be extremely proud.

"Creating Chances is a means of showcasing all of the work that takes place right across the League on a daily basis and will help to further strengthen the relationship we have with countless charities, good causes and our fans."

SHOOTY'S GUIDE TO P

TOP STATS ABOUT TOP STRIKES!

LEDLEY KING
...scored the fastest goal in Prem history. In December 2000, he gave Spurs the lead at Bradford after just ten seconds! You can't even eat a burger in that time!

ROBBIE FOWLER
...scored the fastest ever hat-trick in the Premier League way back in 1994. The former Liverpool hero scored three goals in four minutes and 33 seconds as the Reds beat Arsenal 4-2!

PORTSMOUTH
Eleven goals were scored when Pompey beat Reading 7-4 last month. It was the most goals scored in one Premier League game. That's a goal every eight and a half minutes!

ALAN SHEARER
...is the Prem's top scorer ever. He smacked in 261 goals during his time at Blackburn and Newcastle!

MARK HUGHES
...scored for five different Prem clubs during his playing career – Man United, Chelsea, Southampton, Everton and Blackburn. The Rovers boss should get his boots back on!

TCH...

6 STEVEN GERRARD

HISTORY IS ON STEVIE'S SIDE!

He gave his all in the battle with Chelsea at Anfield. And it's not over yet for Stevie G! The Reds have been in seven Euro semis in the last 43 years – and they've won the lot!

7 WAYNE ROONEY

ROO HAS POINT TO PROVE!

Unhappy at playing out wide in the Nou Camp and then being subbed with 15 minutes to go, expect a wound-up Wazza to be raring to go against Barcelona this week!

8 THEO WALCOTT

TIME TO MAKE HIS MARK!

After finally getting a starting place for the Gunners, Theo's brill performance against Reading was described by boss Arsene Wenger as his best yet in an Arsenal shirt!

NEW ENTRY

9 DAVID BECKHAM

BECKS MAKES LA CONFIDENT!

After a slow start to the US season, Becks is starting to weave his magic once again and he set up both goals as LA Galaxy twice came from behind to draw with Houston!

NEW ENTRY

10 ASHLEY YOUNG

A HERO FOR THE VILLANS!

Two skill goals in the 5-1 derby-day demolition of arch-rivals Birmingham sent Aston Villa fans wild with delight – and will have impressed watching England boss Fabio Capello too!

NEW ENTRY

REM GOALS

JAMES VAUGHAN

The Everton star is the youngest player to score in the Prem – aged 16 years and 271 days – against Crystal Palace on April 10, 2005. He beat James Milner's record by 86 days!

PAUL SCHOLES

...has scored the most Premier League goals from midfield – 96 over 14 seasons. His best season was in 2002/03 when he scored 14. Look out for Scholesy's 100th this season Shootsters!

THIERRY HENRY

...scored 20 goals or more in five seasons in a row for Arsenal! His best season was in 2003/04 when he hit 30!

MAN UNITED

...beat Ipswich 9-0 at Old Trafford in 1995. It is the biggest Premier League win ever and Andy Cole scored five of 'em! Ryan Giggs also scored that day.

JERMAINE PENNANT

When the Liverpool winger was at Arsenal, he and Robert Pires scored hat-tricks in the same game as Arsenal beat Southampton 6-1 in 2003!

GARY SPEED

...has scored in every Prem season. He's netted for Leeds, Everton, Newcastle and now Bolton. Not bad for a midfielder, eh?!

XABI ALONSO

...holds the record for scoring the longest Premier League goal from open play. He scored from 60 metres (that's still inside his own half!) against Newcastle in September, 2006. Hey Shootsters, try that in a game for your team!

HER...

ONLY IN *SHOOT*

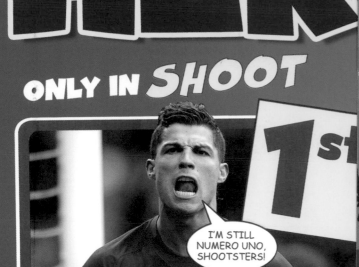

I'M STILL NUMERO UNO, SHOOTSTERS!

1st

CRISTIANO RONALD...

RONNY'S PAIN IN SPAIN MEANS BARCELONA COULD PAY THE PENALTY AT OLD TRAFFORD...

OK, so he may have missed a penalty against Barcelona last week, but the Ronster's still spot on as far as we're concerned! He's been absolutely skill all season for Man United and is easily the best player in the Prem! He doesn't lack the confidence to triumph in Europe either! After failing to find the net at the Nou Camp he made a promise to Reds' fans, saying: "I will now score in the second leg in Manchester!" Barca dudes – you have been warned!

★ **2008** The year at a glance... PREMIER LEA...

The voice of football **SHOOT** **SCOOP!**

THE LIFE OF RYAN

WITH TEN PREMIER League titles and two European Cups safely locked away in his trophy cabinet along with a whole host of other awards, Ryan Giggs is a living legend at Manchester United.

The Old Trafford winger ended his Wales career in May 2007 so he could prolong his club playing days and there is every sign that he's achieved his aim. He's passed the 750 game mark for the club and still counting!
But he's already planning for his future as he's been taking his coaching badges.
But the signs suggest Giggsy could continue at United for at least another season!

GIGGSY ON BEING A PRO

It is hard work being a player?
"There are a lot of plusses to being a professional footballer but you have got to get your rest and watch what you drink. I like to go out and enjoy myself just like the next person but you've got to realise you have to make sacrifices in this job."

GIGGSY ON STARTING OUT

It's been more than 17 years since you started at Man United...
"Back then I could never have dreamed what my career would be like, I just wanted to get into the first team. My years at United have been unbelievable. I've been very fortunate."

★ **2009** The year at a glance... PREMIER LEAGUE WINNERS: Manchester United ★ FA CUP WINNERS: Chelsea

Ryan Giggs has his 35th birthday in November – but he also hopes to be celebrating next May!

GIGGSY ON STAYING FIT

How have you kept going with the game getting faster and players fitter every year?
"I changed a lot of things when I was 30. I knocked alcohol on the head even though I may have the odd glass of wine. I look at my diet too and then there's stuff like yoga and ice baths. I train five per cent harder."

GIGGSY ON STILL PLAYING

What's it like playing now after so long in the game?
"I still get the same buzz out of playing and winning. It's something that never fades and actually increases as you get older."

ROLL OF HONOUR

What Ryan's won

Champions League: 1999, 2008.
Premier League: 1993, 1994, 1995, 1996, 1997, 1999, 2001, 2003, 2007, 2008.
FA Cup: 1994, 1996, 1999, 2004.
League Cup: 1992, 2006.
Community Shield: 1993, 1994, 1996, 1997, 2003, 2007, 2008.
UEFA Super Cup: 1991.
Intercontinental Cup: 1999.
FA Youth Cup: 1992.
Ryan has won many individual awards, including an OBE.

GIGGSY ON RECORDS

Ryan, did you ever set out to create a whole host of personal bests?
"I don't look at personal records but I do look at winning things that have never been done before. When you have been around a while you realise what is at stake, you think this could be your last tournament or last league so you make sure you enjoy it. I probably didn't enjoy 1999 [Champions League win] as much as this year but I made the most of it because those sort of games don't come around very often."

GIGGSY ON BEING AT OLD TRAFFORD

Does it help being with Man United?
"The whole set up at the club is geared to excellence with sports scientists and the medical department. There are no excuses for not preparing yourself for games. I would like to go on but let's see how I feel. Even though I missed a lot of games last season I was still knackered. Now I feel I can play in every game."